SPEAK ENGLISH
LIKE AN AMERICAN

YOU ALREADY SPEAK ENGLISH...
NOW SPEAK IT EVEN BETTER!

DELUXE BOOK & CD SET

AMY GILLETT

LANGUAGE
SUCCESS
PRESS

ANN ARBOR, MICHIGAN

First Edition

ISBN 0-9725300-3-7
Library of Congress Control Number: 2004102958

Visit our website: www.languagesuccesspress.com

Bulk discounts are available. For information, please contact:

Language Success Press
2232 S. Main Street #345
Ann Arbor, MI 48103
USA

E-mail: sales@languagesuccesspress.com
Fax: (303) 484-2004 (USA)

Printed in the United States of America

hit the nail on the head gung ho come to an agreement in that case stand a chance no wonder when pigs fly hang around cup of tea make a f~~ortune~~ ~~deliver~~ the goods get the ball roll~~ing~~ **ACKNOWLEDGEMENTS** ~~wisdom~~ wisdom take something by storm ~~burn the midnight oil~~ you can say that again sweeten the deal get the ball rolling first things first

ACKNOWLEDGEMENTS

The author is very grateful to the following people for their collaboration and advice while preparing this book and CD set: Vijay Banta, Jacqueline Gillett, Thomas Gillett, Marcy Carreras, John McDermott, Natasha McDermott, Cat McGrath, Patrick O'Connell.

ABOUT THE AUTHOR

Amy Gillett has taught English as a Second Language (ESL) in Stamford, Connecticut and in Prague, Czech Republic. Her essays and humor writing have appeared in many publications, including *MAD Magazine*, the *San Francisco Chronicle*, and *Family Circle*. Amy majored in Slavic Languages and Literature at Stanford University and holds a Master's degree from Stanford in Russian and Eastern European Studies.

Amy has studied and worked abroad in many countries and speaks several foreign languages, including Russian, Czech, French, and Italian. She is also the author of *Speak English Like an American for Native Spanish Speakers*, *Speak English Like an American for Native Russian Speakers*, and *Speak English Like an American for Native Japanese Speakers*.

ABOUT THE ILLUSTRATOR

Manny José is an illustrator and graphic designer who has been doodling and sketching for as long as he can remember. He is from Toronto, Canada and currently lives in Brooklyn, New York. For more of Manny's illustrations, visit www.mannytoons.com.

TABLE OF CONTENTS

hit the nail on the head gung ho come to an agreement in that case stand a chance no wonder when pigs fly hang around cup of tea make ... goods get the ball ro... ...sdom take something by storm burn the midnight oil you can say that again sweeten the deal get the ball rolling first things first

INTRODUCTION..7
MAIN CHARACTERS..9

LESSON 1: Bob's Day at Work..11
LESSON 2: Bob Returns Home with Bad News....................17
LESSON 3: Ted's Day at School..23
LESSON 4: Nicole's Day at School.......................................27
LESSON 5: Ted Goes Out for the Evening............................33
REVIEW: LESSONS 1-5..37

LESSON 6: Susan Stays Home and Bakes Cookies...............41
LESSON 7: Susan Hires Bob to Run Her Business................47
LESSON 8: Ted Forms a Rock Band.....................................51
LESSON 9: Nicole For President!..57
LESSON 10: Bob Visits the Village Market............................63
REVIEW: LESSONS 6-10..67

LESSON 11: Bob Drives a Hard Bargain.................................71
LESSON 12: Bob's Big Cookie Order......................................75
LESSON 13: Amber Comes Over to Bake Cookies..................81
LESSON 14: Amber and Ted Heat Up the Kitchen...................87
LESSON 15: Nicole Practices Her Election Speech..................93
REVIEW: LESSONS 11-15...98

LESSON 16: Bob Brings the Cookies to the Village Market...101

LESSON 17: Carol Tells Bob the Good News..........................105

LESSON 18: Everyone Bakes Cookies....................................111

LESSON 19: Nicole's Close Election.....................................117

LESSON 20: Bob Gets an Angry Call from Carol...................121

REVIEW: LESSONS 16-20..125

LESSON 21: Susan Gets a Surprise Call................................129

LESSON 22: Susan Shares the Good News...........................133

LESSON 23: Bob Has a Surprise Visitor................................139

LESSON 24: Amber Writes a Song.......................................145

LESSON 25: Ted Brings Home More Good News..................151

REVIEW: LESSONS 21-25..155

CHALLENGE CROSSWORD PUZZLE.................................158

ANSWER KEY..160

INDEX..169

hit the nail on the head gung ho come to an agreement in that case stand a chance no wonder when pigs fly hang around cup of tea make

INTRODUCTION

e goods get the ball rolling the onal wisdom take something by storm burn the midnight oil you can say that

If you already speak some English and now would like to speak more like a native, you've found the right book. One of the keys to speaking like a native is the ability to use and understand casual expressions, or idioms. American English is full of idioms. You won't learn these expressions in a standard textbook. But you will hear them all the time in everyday conversations. You'll also meet them in books, newspapers, magazines, and TV shows. This book will help you understand and use idioms better. It contains over 300 of today's most common idioms.

Idioms add color to the language. Master idioms and your speech will be less awkward, less foreign. You'll also understand more of what you read and hear. Often a student of English tries to translate idioms word-for-word, or literally. If you do this, you can end up asking, "What could this possibly mean?" This is why idioms are difficult: they work as groups of words, not as individual words. If you translate each word on its own, you'll miss the meaning and in many cases end up with nonsense.

As an example, let's take one of the idioms presented in this book: "out of this world." This expression is often used to describe delicious food. If you have a party and you serve a delicious chicken dish, your American friend might tell you, "This chicken is out of this world!" Start translating the expression word-for-word and you'll have to ask yourself: "What world is it in?" and "Why is she even commenting on the chicken being in a world, *any* world?"

Here's another example. Let's say you're on a tennis team. Your team has won every single game for the past six months. You could tell your friend this without using an idiom: "Our team is lucky because we keep winning game after game." You can also express this with an idiom: "Our team is on a winning streak." Sounds better, doesn't it?

When using idioms, remember that their word order and structure are often *not* flexible. In other words, you will need to get the word order exactly right. Here's an example of what I mean. Recently, I helped a student with his English homework. He then told me, "You've got a golden heart." He was trying to speak idiomatic English, but the correct expression is: "You've got a heart of gold."

This book includes a CD of all of the dialogues. The CD will help you with pronunciation and will also help you remember the idioms. Play it at home, at work, in the car, while traveling…before you know it, you'll be speaking English like an American!

Try to "develop an ear" for idioms on your own. Don't worry, I'm not suggesting you try to grow a third ear! "Develop an ear" is an idiom — it means to learn to listen for something. If you don't know what an expression means, ask a native speaker of English. Here's what you can say to your helper: *Excuse me, I ran across this expression and I'm not sure what it means. Can you please help me out?*

Add idioms to your speech and writing just as you add vocabulary. You may find it helpful to write all of the expressions in this book down on notecards and review them whenever you have a free moment.

Good luck adding idioms to your everyday speech. It's fun, and you'll enjoy speaking English much more. Like an American!

CR

MAIN CHARACTERS

The author would like to thank the Johnson family for graciously agreeing to appear in this book.

The Johnson Family

Ted (*son*)

Bob (*father*)

Nicole (*daughter*)

Susan (*mother*)

BOB'S DAY AT WORK

Bob works as a manager in a furniture store. Peter, his boss, is not happy about sales. Bob's new advertising campaign hasn't helped. Peter decides to fire him.

Peter: Bob, I hate to **break the news**, but our sales were down again last month.

Bob: Down again, Peter?

Peter: Yeah. These days, everybody's shopping at our competition, Honest Abe's Furniture Store.

Bob: But everything in there **costs an arm and a leg**!

Peter: That's true. They do charge **top dollar**.

Bob: And their salespeople are very strange. They really **give me the creeps**!

Peter: Well, they must be doing something right over there. Meanwhile, we're **about to go belly-up**.

Bob: I'm sorry to hear that. I thought my new advertising campaign would **save the day**.

Peter: **Let's face it**: your advertising campaign was a **real flop**.

Bob: Well then I'll **go back to the drawing board**.

Peter: It's too late for that. You're fired!

Bob: What? You're **giving me the ax**?

Peter: Yes. I've already found a new manager. She's as **sharp as a tack**.

Bob: Can't we even **talk this over**? **After all**, I've been working here for 10 years!

Peter: There's **no point in** arguing, Bob. I've already **made up my mind**.

Bob: Oh well, **at least** I won't have to **put up with** your nonsense anymore! Good-bye to you and good-bye to this **dead-end job**.

Peter: Please leave before I **lose my temper**!

IDIOMS – LESSON 1

about to – ready to; on the verge of

EXAMPLE 1: It's a good thing Bob left the furniture store when he did. Peter was so angry, he was **about to** throw a dining room chair at him.
EXAMPLE 2: I'm glad you're finally home. I was just **about to** have dinner without you.

after all – despite everything; when everything has been considered; the fact is

EXAMPLE 1: You'd better invite Ed to your party. **After all**, he's a good friend.
EXAMPLE 2: It doesn't matter what your boss thinks of you. **After all**, you're going to quit your job anyway.

at least – anyway; the *good* thing is that...

EXAMPLE 1: We've run out of coffee, but **at least** we still have tea.
EXAMPLE 2: Tracy can't afford to buy a car, but **at least** she has a good bicycle.

NOTE: The second definition of this phrase is "no less than": There were **at least** 300 people waiting in line to buy concert tickets.

(to) break the news – to make something known

EXAMPLE 1: Samantha and Michael are getting married, but they haven't yet **broken the news** to their parents.

EXAMPLE 2: You'd better **break the news** to your father carefully. After all, you don't want him to have a heart attack!

(to) cost an arm and a leg – to be very expensive

EXAMPLE 1: A college education in America **costs an arm and a leg**.

EXAMPLE 2: All of the furniture at Honest Abe's **costs an arm and a leg**!

dead-end job – a job that won't lead to anything else

EXAMPLE 1: Diane realized that working as a cashier was a **dead-end job**.

EXAMPLE 2: Jim worked many **dead-end jobs** before finally deciding to start his own business.

(let's) face it – accept a difficult reality

EXAMPLE 1: **Let's face it**, if Ted spent more time studying, he wouldn't be failing so many of his classes!

EXAMPLE 2: **Let's face it**, if you don't have a college degree, it can be difficult to find a high-paying job.

(to) give one the creeps – to create a feeling of disgust or horror

EXAMPLE 1: Ted's friend Matt has seven earrings in each ear and an "I Love Mom" tattoo on his arm. He really **gives Nicole the creeps**.

EXAMPLE 2: There was a strange man following me around the grocery store. He was **giving me the creeps**!

(to) go back to the drawing board – to start a task over because the last try failed; to start again from the beginning

EXAMPLE 1: Frank's new business failed, so he had to **go back to the drawing board**.

EXAMPLE 2: The president didn't agree with our new ideas for the company, so we had to **go back to the drawing board**.

(to) go belly-up – to go bankrupt

EXAMPLE 1: Many people lost their jobs when Enron **went belly-up**.

EXAMPLE 2: My company lost $3 million last year. We might go **belly-up**.

(to) give someone the ax – to fire someone

EXAMPLE 1: Mary used to talk to her friends on the phone all day at work, until one day her boss finally **gave her the ax**.

EXAMPLE 2: Poor Paul! He was **given the ax** two days before Christmas.

(to) lose one's temper – to become very angry

EXAMPLE 1: Bob always **loses his temper** when his kids start talking on the telephone during dinner.

EXAMPLE 2: When Ted handed in his essay two weeks late, his teacher really **lost her temper.**

(to) make up one's mind – to reach a decision; to decide

EXAMPLE 1: Stephanie couldn't **make up her mind** whether to attend Harvard or Stanford. Finally, she chose Stanford.

EXAMPLE 2: Do you want an omelette or fried eggs? You'll need to **make up your mind** quickly because the waitress is coming.

no point in – no reason to; it's not worth (doing something)

EXAMPLE 1: There's **no point in** worrying about things you can't change.

EXAMPLE 2: There's **no point in** going on a picnic if it's going to rain.

(to) put up with – to endure without complaint

EXAMPLE 1: For many years, Barbara **put up with** her husband's annoying behavior. Finally, she decided to leave him.

EXAMPLE 2: I don't know how Len **puts up with** his mean boss every day.

real flop *or* **flop** – a failure

EXAMPLE 1: The Broadway play closed after just 4 days – it was a **real flop!**

EXAMPLE 2: The company was in trouble after its new product **flopped.**

(to) save the day – to prevent a disaster or misfortune

EXAMPLE 1: The Christmas tree was on fire, but Ted threw water on it and **saved the day.**

EXAMPLE 2: We forgot to buy champagne for our New Year's party, but Sonia brought some and really **saved the day!**

(as) sharp as a tack – very intelligent

EXAMPLE 1: Jay scored 100% on his science test. He's as **sharp as a tack.**

EXAMPLE 2: Anna got a scholarship to Yale. She's as **sharp as a tack.**

(to) talk over – to discuss

EXAMPLE 1: Dave and I spent hours **talking over** the details of the plan.

EXAMPLE 2: Before you make any big decisions, give me a call and we'll **talk things over.**

top dollar – the highest end of a price range; a lot of money

EXAMPLE 1: Nicole paid **top dollar** for a shirt at Banana Republic.

EXAMPLE 2: Wait until those jeans go on sale. Why pay **top dollar**?

☙ Practice the Idioms

Fill in the blank with the missing word:

1) I can't believe you bought a couch at Honest Abe's. Everything in that store costs an arm and a _____.

    a) foot   b) leg   c) hand

2) After Bob found out that his advertising campaign failed, he wanted to go back to the drawing _____.

    a) board   b) table   c) room

3) When somebody isn't listening to you, there's no _____ in trying to argue with them.

    a) edge   b) tip   c) point

4) José is really smart. He's as sharp as a _____.

    a) tack   b) nail   c) screw

5) The salespeople at Honest Abe's always look angry and never speak to anybody. No wonder they _____ Bob the creeps.

    a) take   b) give   c) allow

6) Bob got fired. He isn't looking forward to _____ the news to his family.

    a) breaking   b) cracking   c) saying

7) Bob thought his new advertisements would bring in lots of customers and save the _____.

    a) morning   b) night   c) day

8) Fortunately, Bob no longer has to put _____ with his stupid boss at the furniture store.

    a) over   b) in   c) up

ANSWERS TO LESSON 1, p. 160

BOB RETURNS HOME WITH BAD NEWS

Bob tells his wife Susan that he lost his job. Susan suggests that he start his own business.

Susan: **What's the matter**, dear?

Bob: Susan, I **got canned** today at work.

Susan: But Bob, you were Peter's **right-hand man**!

Bob: Yes, and he **stabbed me in the back**.

Susan: **Keep your chin up**. Maybe he'll **change his mind** and take you back.

Bob: **When pigs fly**! Once he **makes up his mind,** he never changes it. Besides, I **told him off**.

Susan: **Look on the bright side**: you won't have to **set eyes** on Peter ever again.

Bob: **Thank goodness** for that!

Susan: **Hang in there**. I'm sure you won't be **out of work** for long.

Bob: In the meantime, we'll have to **live from hand to mouth**.

Susan: Don't get too **stressed out,** Bob. We'll **make ends meet**.

Bob: I can always get a job at McDonald's as a **last resort**.

Susan: I don't think they're hiring right now.

Bob: If **worse comes to worst,** we can sell our home and move into a tent.

Susan: Let's **think big!** Maybe you can start your own business.

Bob: **Easier said than done!**

IDIOMS – LESSON 2

(to) change one's mind – to change one's opinion or decision

EXAMPLE 1: Brandon wasn't going to take a vacation this year, but then he **changed his mind** and went to Bora Bora for two weeks.
EXAMPLE 2: Why aren't you applying to medical school this year? Did you **change your mind** about becoming a doctor?

easier said than done – more difficult than you think

EXAMPLE 1: You want to climb Mount Everest? **Easier said than done!**
EXAMPLE 2: Moving into a new home is **easier said than done.**

(to) get canned [slang] – to lose one's job; to get fired

EXAMPLE 1: After Chris **got canned,** it took him a year to find a new job.
EXAMPLE 2: Lisa is a lousy secretary. She deserves to **get canned!**
SYNONYMS: to get sacked; to be given the ax

(to) hang in there – to persevere; to not give up

EXAMPLE 1: I know you're four games behind, but you can still win the tennis match. Just **hang in there!**
EXAMPLE 2: **Hang in there,** Don! Your invention will soon be a success.

if worse comes to worst – in the worst case; if absolutely necessary

EXAMPLE 1: Ted's car isn't running well. **If worse comes to worst,** he can take the bus to school.
EXAMPLE 2: I know you're running out of money. **If worse comes to worst,** you can always sell some of your jewelry.

(to) keep one's chin up – to stay positive

EXAMPLE 1: Even when he was unemployed and homeless, Bill managed to **keep his chin up**.

EXAMPLE 2: **Keep your chin up!** You'll find your lost dog soon.

last resort – if there are no other alternatives left; the last solution for getting out of a difficulty

EXAMPLE 1: David was locked out of his house. He knew that as a **last resort**, he could always break a window.

EXAMPLE 2: I don't like taking medicine. I'll only take it as a **last resort**.

(to) live from hand to mouth – to barely have enough money to survive

EXAMPLE 1: Jenny was earning $5 an hour working at the store. She was really **living from hand to mouth**.

EXAMPLE 2: George is really poor. He **lives from hand to mouth**.

(to) look on the bright side – to be optimistic; to think about the positive part or aspect of a situation

EXAMPLE 1: Leo was upset that his soccer game was canceled. His mother said, "**Look on the bright side**, now you can stay home and watch TV."

EXAMPLE 2: You lost your job? **Look on the bright side**, now you'll have more free time!

(to) make ends meet – to manage one's money so as to have enough to live on; to be okay financially

EXAMPLE 1: Kimberly wasn't able to **make ends meet** so she had to ask her parents to pay her rent.

EXAMPLE 2: If you can't **make ends meet**, you'll need to start spending less.

(to) make up one's mind – *see Lesson 1*

out of work – unemployed; not working

EXAMPLE 1: Gary was **out of work** for a year before finding a new job.

EXAMPLE 2: Bob is **out of work**. Do you know anybody who might want to hire him?

right-hand man – the most helpful assistant or employee

EXAMPLE 1: Juan's **right-hand man** helps him make all of his decisions.

EXAMPLE 2: When Jack Thompson retired as president of his company, his **right-hand man** took over.

(to) set eyes on – to look at; to see for the first time

EXAMPLE 1: Ted was in love from the moment he **set eyes on** Amber.
EXAMPLE 2: Susan knew from the moment she **set eyes on** Ted's friend Lucas that he would be trouble.

(to) stab someone in the back – to betray someone

EXAMPLE 1: Jill and Heather were friends, until Heather **stabbed Jill in the back** by stealing her boyfriend.
EXAMPLE 2: You're firing me after all I've done for this company? You're really **stabbing me in the back!**

(to be) stressed out – under severe strain; very anxious

EXAMPLE 1: Al is so **stressed out** about his job that he can't sleep at night.
EXAMPLE 2: You've been so **stressed out** lately. You really need to take a long vacation!

(to) tell off – to scold; to tell someone in strong words what one really thinks

EXAMPLE 1: When Ted showed up for chemistry class a half an hour late, his teacher really **told him off**.
EXAMPLE 2: Patty is going to **tell off** the plumber because the pipes he said he fixed are still leaking.

thank goodness – I'm grateful; I'm relieved

EXAMPLE 1: When Ted came home at 4 a.m. last Sunday, his mother said, "**Thank goodness** you're home! I was so worried about you."
EXAMPLE 2: **Thank goodness** you didn't go to California on Monday. It rained there every day this week.

(to) think big – to set high goals

EXAMPLE 1: Why run for Governor of New York? **Think big**: run for President of the United States!
EXAMPLE 2: Ken and Sandra hope to sell their house for $3 million dollars. They always **think big**.

What's the matter? – What's the problem?

EXAMPLE 1: **What's the matter**, Bob? You don't look very happy.
EXAMPLE 2: Oscar looks very pale. **What's the matter** with him?

When pigs fly! [slang] – never

EXAMPLE 1: Will Ted teach Nicole how to play the guitar? **When pigs fly!**
EXAMPLE 2: Sure, I'll give you my new laptop. **When pigs fly!**
SYNONYMS: when hell freezes over; never in a million years

❧ PRACTICE THE IDIOMS

Fill in the blank with the missing word:

1) What's the _____? You look upset.

   a) situation   b) issue   c) matter

2) I know I can trust you. You would never stab me in the _____.

   a) leg   b) back   c) arm

3) If Bob and Susan run out of money, they can always borrow money from Susan's sister as a _____ resort.

   a) final   b) first   c) last

4) You look really stressed _____. Why don't you sit down, relax, and have a cup of tea?

   a) about   b) in   c) out

5) Bob, everything will be fine. You just need to keep your chin _____ and remember that tomorrow is another day.

   a) up   b) down   c) above

6) I just can't make up my _____ whether to order chicken or fish.

   a) head   b) brain   c) mind

7) Nicole accidentally stepped on Ted's guitar. Ted got really angry and told her _____.

   a) off   b) out   c) away

8) Your husband left you for his psychologist? Hang ____ there! I'm sure he'll realize she's crazy and then come back to you.

   a) up   b) in   c) out

ANSWERS TO LESSON 2, p. 160

Ted's chemistry class is way over his head.

TED'S DAY AT SCHOOL

Ted tells his parents he did poorly on his chemistry test. They tell him he needs to get serious and study more.

Susan: How was your day at school today, Ted?

Ted: Bad. I had a chemistry test, and I **blew it**!

Susan: Maybe if you didn't **cut class** so often, you'd do better.

Bob: That's right, son. Stop **slacking off** and start **hitting the books**!

Ted: But I **can't stand** chemistry class. Besides, it's a **lost cause**. That class is way **over my head**.

Susan: You need to **buckle down**.

Ted: When I'm a famous musician, people won't **give a hoot** about my knowledge of atoms and molecules.

Bob: That's **beside the point.**

Susan: We know you have your **heart set on** going to New York University.

Bob: And you don't **stand a chance** of getting in there with such poor grades!

IDIOMS – LESSON 3

beside the point – not relevant; not important

EXAMPLE 1: Whether or not I asked the waiter to bring us water is **beside the point**. Waiters should always bring water to the table.
EXAMPLE 2: The reason you're late is **beside the point**. The fact is, your dinner is now cold.

(to) blow something – to spoil or botch something

EXAMPLE 1: Brenda **blew the interview** and didn't get the job offer.
EXAMPLE 2: Randy managed to get a date with the most popular girl in his class. Now I hope he doesn't **blow it**!

(to) buckle down – to start working seriously

EXAMPLE 1: If Don **buckles down** now, he might be able to graduate from high school this year.
EXAMPLE 2: Team, if we want to win this tournament, we're going to need to **buckle down**!

can't stand – to hate

EXAMPLE 1: Bob **can't stand** bureaucrats, so he'd never do well working at a large corporation.
EXAMPLE 2: Nicole **can't stand** broccoli. She simply refuses to eat it.

(to) cut class – to miss class without an excuse

EXAMPLE 1: Ted often **cuts class** to spend more time with his girlfriend.
EXAMPLE 2: If you keep **cutting French class**, you're going to fail it.

Get real! – be serious or realistic about what's going on

EXAMPLE 1: You think you won't get a speeding ticket when you drive 85 miles per hour? **Get real!**
EXAMPLE 2: You think you're going to win $1 million in the lottery? **Get real!**

(to) have one's heart set on – to really want something

EXAMPLE 1: Nicole **has her heart set on** going to New York this weekend.
EXAMPLE 2: Did you really **have your heart set on** going to Harvard?

(to) hit the books – to start studying

EXAMPLE 1: Ted partied all weekend. Finally, on Sunday night, he decided it was time to **hit the books**.
EXAMPLE 2: **Hit the books!** I know you have a test tomorrow.

lost cause – something hopeless

EXAMPLE 1: Cindy spent five years studying Russian. Finally, she realized it was a **lost cause**. She would never learn it.
EXAMPLE 2: Jack needs to stop drinking so much coffee, but he's so addicted to caffeine that it's a **lost cause**.

(to) not give a hoot – to not care about

EXAMPLE 1: Tom likes to walk around town in his pajamas — he doesn't **give a hoot** what people think.
EXAMPLE 2: Stephanie **doesn't give a hoot** if she's the only one wearing a green dress to the high school prom.

SYNONYMS: to not give a damn; to not give a darn

over one's head – beyond one's understanding

EXAMPLE 1: The professor was **speaking over our heads**. None of us could understand him.
EXAMPLE 2: The article on cloning was written for scientists. It was **over my head**.

(to) slack off – to waste time

EXAMPLE 1: Amanda doesn't get much done at the office. She's too busy **slacking off**.
EXAMPLE 2: I'd better stop **slacking off**. My essay is due in two hours.

NOTE: People who **slack off** all the time are called "slackers."

(to) stand a chance – to have the possibility of success

EXAMPLE 1: Although the American figure skaters were good, they didn't **stand a chance** of winning a gold medal at the Olympics.
EXAMPLE 2: Wilton High School has the best soccer team in the state. I'm afraid we don't **stand a chance** against them!

✎ PRACTICE THE IDIOMS

Choose the most appropriate reply to the following statements:

1) *Bob:* "Susan, I can't get my old job back. It's a lost cause."
   Susan's reply:
   a) "Lost? Maybe I can help you find it."
   b) "Yes, I know it's not a good cause."
   c) "I understand. You'll find something else."

2) *Susan:* "How could Peter fire you? Were you slacking off?"
   Bob's reply:
       a) "No. I was working very hard!"
       b) "No. I talked on the phone to friends all day."
       c) "Yes. I was working very hard!"

3) *Ted:* "It's getting late. I'd better start hitting the books."
   Bob's reply:
       a) "Yes, that's a good idea. Spend some time studying."
       b) "Hit the books? Why don't you read them instead?"
       c) "Why don't you study instead?"

4) *Peter:* "I don't give a hoot how long you've been working here."
   Bob's reply:
       a) "I wouldn't give you a hoot either."
       b) "I guess our years together aren't important to you."
       c) "Yes, it was a long time."

5) *Bob:* "Susan, the truth is that I couldn't stand Peter."
   Susan's reply:
       a) "I know. Peter really liked you too."
       b) "I liked him too. He was a nice guy."
       c) "I didn't like him either. He was a jerk."

6) *Susan:* "Nicole, do you ever cut class?"
   Nicole's reply:
       a) "No. I've never missed a single class."
       b) "Yes. I had to leave my math class early yesterday."
       c) "No. Sometimes I go to the mall during class time."

7) *Bob:* "This book on computers is way over my head."
   Susan's reply:
       a) "Over your head? It should be in front of your face!"
       b) "Why don't you start with an easier book?"
       c) "Here, try this book. It's more difficult."

8) *Nicole:* "I've got my heart set on going to the school picnic."
   Susan's reply:
       a) "Okay. You should definitely go."
       b) "Really? Why don't you want to go?"
       c) "I understand. Picnics can be boring."

ANSWERS TO LESSON 3, p. 160

NICOLE'S DAY AT SCHOOL

Nicole tells her mother Susan about her successful presentation at school. Her brother Ted overhears and interrupts the conversation.

Susan: How was your day at school today, Nicole?

Nicole: It was great, Mom. I gave a presentation on Hillary Clinton in government class. Afterwards, my teacher **paid me a compliment**.

Susan: What did she say?

Nicole: She said my presentation was **head and shoulders above** the others.

Susan: **Way to go**!

Nicole: She also said I should **go into** politics, just like Hillary.

Ted: You're so **gung ho** about school. It **drives me crazy**.

Nicole: Ted, don't **butt in**! You're just jealous.

Ted: Right. You **hit the nail on the head**. I'm **green with envy**.

Nicole: Would you just **shut up**? You're **on thin ice with** me right now.

Ted: Oh no! Look at me. I'm **shaking in my shoes**!

IDIOMS – LESSON 4

(to) butt in [slang] – to interrupt; to interfere

EXAMPLE 1: Nancy is always **butting in** to other people's business.
EXAMPLE 2: Sara is really rude. She always **butts in** to other people's conversations.

(to) drive one crazy – to annoy someone very much

EXAMPLE 1: Don't ask Mrs. Smith how old she is. It **drives her crazy**.
EXAMPLE 2: Please stop chewing gum so loudly. It's **driving me crazy**!
SYNONYMS: to drive one nuts; to drive one up the wall

(to) go into – to enter a profession

EXAMPLE 1: Lisa enjoys arguing with people, so she decided to **go into** law.
EXAMPLE 2: Do you like solving people's problems? If so, you should consider **going into** psychology.

NOTE: "Go into" has several other meanings, including:
1. Enter. **Go into** the house and get a pen.
2. Enter another emotional state. Sally **went into** hysterics.
3. Discuss details. I don't have time now to **go into** the whole story.

green with envy – desiring another's advantages or things

EXAMPLE 1: When Daniel got promoted to vice president of the bank, his colleagues were **green with envy**.
EXAMPLE 2: You won the lottery? I'm **green with envy**!

gung ho – very enthusiastic; very excited (about something)

EXAMPLE 1: Heather is really **gung ho** about her new job.
EXAMPLE 2: Sharon really loves college. She's very **gung ho**.

NOTE: If the expression "gung ho" doesn't sound like English to you, there's a reason. It comes from a Mandarin Chinese phrase meaning "working together." A US Marine Corps commander in China adopted this expression as the motto for his battalion during World War 2 and from there it sailed over to the United States and came into common use.

head and shoulders above – far superior to

EXAMPLE 1: The Boston Symphony Orchestra is **head and shoulders above** any other orchestra in the area.
EXAMPLE 2: I can't believe you only won second prize in the competition. You were **head and shoulders above** the first-prize winner!

(to) hit the nail on the head – to be right

EXAMPLE 1: Dawn **hit the nail on the head** when she said that Tiffany is jealous of Amber.
EXAMPLE 2: Steve **hit the nail on the head** with his idea of moving his company's manufacturing facility to China.

(to be) on thin ice (with someone) – to be in a dangerous position; to be temporarily on somebody's bad side

EXAMPLE 1: Joey was **on thin ice** with his mom after he spent his lunch money on candy bars.
EXAMPLE 2: Bill was **on thin ice** with his girlfriend after she saw him at the movie theater with another girl.

NOTE: There is also the variation "to skate on thin ice." Joey knew he was **skating on thin ice** when he bought candy with his lunch money.

(to) pay (someone) a compliment – to give someone a compliment; to offer someone an admiring comment

EXAMPLE 1: Professor Russo **paid Jennifer a compliment**. He said she had a beautiful smile.
EXAMPLE 2: Isn't it wonderful to **pay someone a compliment**? It makes them feel good, and it doesn't cost you anything!

(to) shake in one's shoes – to tremble with fear; to be afraid

EXAMPLE 1: Brianna is scared of her French teacher, Monsieur Le Monstre. Whenever he speaks to her, Brianna starts **shaking in her shoes**.
EXAMPLE 2: During the storm, Billy was hiding under his kitchen table and was really **shaking in his shoes**.

shut up
1) be quiet, stop speaking

EXAMPLE: The professor talked for hours. I thought he'd never **shut up**.

2) Stop speaking!

EXAMPLE: Nicole kept telling Ted to turn down his stereo. Finally, he got angry and said, "**Shut up!**"

NOTE: Remember that telling somebody to "shut up!" is rude. It's better to say "Be quiet!" or more politely, "Please be quiet!"

Way to go! – Good work!

EXAMPLE 1: You won $2,000 in the poetry writing contest? **Way to go!**
EXAMPLE 2: That was an interesting article you wrote. **Way to go!**

✎ PRACTICE THE IDIOMS

Fill in the blank with the missing word:

1) Nicole is in a good mood because her teacher _____ her a compliment.

    a) told   b) paid   c) provided

2) Nicole's teacher told her she was _____ and shoulders above her classmates.

    a) elbow   b) neck   c) head

3) When my friend Chad told me he'd just won the lottery, I was _____ with envy.

    a) blue   b) green   c) red

4) When you do something well, your boss might tell you, "Way _____!"

    a) to come   b) to go   c) to act

5) When the robbers entered my house, I was in the kitchen shaking in my _____.

    a) slippers   b) pajamas   c) shoes

6) If somebody is bothering you, you can tell them they're driving you _____.

    a) crazy   b) angry   c) unhappy

7) If you like power, you might consider going _____ politics.

    a) above   b) towards   c) into

8) "You've been yelling and screaming for the past two hours. Could you just shut _____ already?"

    a) up   b) in   c) off

✪ Bonus Practice

Choose the best substitute for the phrase or sentence in bold:

1) When her friend Anna got into Yale, Nicole was **green with envy**.
   a) sick
   b) happy for her
   c) very jealous

2) Bob and Susan are really **gung ho** about the TV show *Survivor*. They watch it every Thursday night.
   a) enthusiastic
   b) concerned
   c) angry

3) **Shut up!** I can't take any more of your screaming.
   a) Talk louder!
   b) Be quiet!
   c) Get out!

4) You got a scholarship to attend Harvard? **Way to go!**
   a) Too bad!
   b) Good work!
   c) Oh well!

5) Please don't **butt in**! We weren't talking to you.
   a) look at us
   b) disagree with us
   c) interrupt our conversation

6) These cookies aren't very good. I think you **hit the nail on the head** when you said I should add more sugar next time.
   a) were wrong
   b) were right
   c) were confused

ANSWERS TO LESSON 4, p. 160

31

TED GOES OUT FOR THE EVENING

Ted leaves to go visit his girlfriend Amber. Ted's mother Susan says she doesn't really like Amber. She wishes him a good time anyway.

Ted: See you later, Mom!

Susan: Where are you going, Ted?

Ted: I told Amber I'd **drop by**.

Susan: What are you two going to do?

Ted: Maybe go to the movies or to a party. Our plans are still **up in the air**.

Susan: Why don't you invite her over here?

Ted: I don't want to **hang around** here. Dad is really **down in the dumps**.

Susan: Is Amber the girl with the nose ring and the purple hair?

Ted: Yeah. I'm **crazy about** her!

Susan: Don't **take this the wrong way**, but she's not exactly my **cup of tea**.

Ted: **Take it easy**, Mom. We're not **about to** get married. We just enjoy **hanging out** together.

Susan: I guess **there's no accounting for taste. Have a good time.**

Ted: Don't worry. We'll **have a blast!**

Susan: (**under her breath**) That's what I'm afraid of!

IDIOMS – LESSON 5

about to – *see Lesson 1*

(to be) crazy about – to like very much

EXAMPLE 1: Amy is so **crazy about** golf, she'd like to play every day.
EXAMPLE 2: I'm sure Katie will agree to go out on a date with Sam. She's **crazy about** him!

cup of tea – the type of person or thing that one generally likes

EXAMPLE 1: Hockey isn't Alan's **cup of tea**. He prefers soccer.
EXAMPLE 2: I know Joy is nice, but she's simply **not my cup of tea**.

NOTE: This expression is almost always used in the negative. She's **not my cup of tea**.

(to be) down in the dumps – to feel sad; to be depressed

EXAMPLE 1: It's not surprising that Lisa is **down in the dumps**. Paws, the cat she had for 20 years, just died.
EXAMPLE 2: It's easy to feel **down in the dumps** when it's raining outside.

(to) drop by – to pay a short, often unannounced visit

EXAMPLE 1: If we have time before the movie, let's **drop by** Bill's house.
EXAMPLE 2: "Hi, I was in the neighborhood so I thought I'd **drop by!**"

(to) hang around – to spend time idly; to linger

EXAMPLE 1: We had to **hang around** the airport for an extra six hours because our flight was delayed.
EXAMPLE 2: Nina's boyfriend Boris is coming over soon. She hopes her parents aren't planning on **hanging around** the house.

(to) hang out – to spend time (often doing nothing)

EXAMPLE 1: Ted spent all of last summer **hanging out** by his friend's pool.
EXAMPLE 2: Kathy and her friends like to **hang out** at the mall.

NOTE: "Hang out with" means to keep company with someone.

(to) have a blast [slang] – to enjoy oneself very much

EXAMPLE 1: Last summer, Nicole **had a blast** backpacking through Europe with some friends.
EXAMPLE 2: Heather spent her spring break in Fort Lauderdale with millions of other college students. She **had a blast**!

(to) have a good time – to enjoy oneself

EXAMPLE 1: Marcy and José **had a good time** salsa dancing at Babalu, a nightclub in Manhattan.
EXAMPLE 2: Nora and Jake **had a good time** on their honeymoon in Maui.

take it easy – relax; don't worry

EXAMPLE 1: You lost your keys? **Take it easy**, I'm sure you'll find them.
EXAMPLE 2: Stop yelling and **take it easy**. I'm sure there's a good explanation for why Joe borrowed your car without asking first.

(to) take something the wrong way – to take offense

EXAMPLE 1: Don't **take this the wrong way**, but I liked your hair better before you got it cut.
EXAMPLE 2: Jessica is offended. I guess she **took it the wrong way** when I told her she should exercise more.

NOTE: This expression is often used in the negative form: "Don't take this the wrong way, but…"

there's no accounting for taste – it's impossible to explain individual likes and dislikes

EXAMPLE 1: Ted likes to put sugar on his spaghetti. I guess **there's no accounting for taste**.
EXAMPLE 2: Tiffany has a tattoo of a squirrel on her leg. **There's no accounting for taste**.

under one's breath – quietly; in a whisper

EXAMPLE 1: "Amber is strange," muttered Nicole **under her breath**, as Ted was leaving the room.
EXAMPLE 2: Mike agreed to take out the garbage, saying **under his breath**, "I always do the dirty work around here."

(to be) up in the air – not yet determined; uncertain

EXAMPLE 1: It might rain later, so our plans for the picnic are **up in the air**.
EXAMPLE 2: Our trip to Russia is **up in the air**. We aren't sure we'll get our visas in time.

✎ PRACTICE THE IDIOMS

Fill in the blank with the missing word:

1) Bob was fired. It's not surprising that he's down ____ the dumps.

   a) at   b) in   c) with

2) Ted thinks Amber is wonderful. He's just crazy ____ her.

   a) about   b) around   c) into

3) "Don't ____ this the wrong way, but I really don't like your girlfriend," said Susan to Ted.

   a) understand   b) put   c) take

4) Ted likes to hang ____ with Amber. She's fun to be with.

   a) on   b) out   c) in

5) Ted decided to go over to Amber's house. He'd promised her he'd drop ____.

   a) by   b) around   c) near

6) Bob and Susan don't know where they'll go on vacation. Their travel plans are still up ____ the air.

   a) around   b) in   c) above

7) Judy muttered something nasty ____ her breath, but I couldn't quite hear it.

   a) about   b) under   c) below

8) Why are you hanging ____ the house on such a beautiful day? You should be outside enjoying the weather.

   a) inside   b) from   c) around

ANSWERS TO LESSON 5, p. 160

Review for Lessons 1-5

Fill in the blank with the missing word:

1) After copying from his friend's paper during the test, Ted was on _____ ice with his chemistry teacher.

   a) thick   b) thin   c) dangerous

2) Ted's teacher hit the _____ on the head. Ted should spend less time playing guitar and more time studying.

   a) tack   b) nail   c) screw

3) I'm not really crazy about my friend's husband. He talks too much, and he never listens to what anybody else is saying. He's just not my cup of _____.

   a) coffee   b) cocoa   c) tea

4) If Ted has his _____ set on going to New York University, he's going to have to buckle down and start studying more.

   a) life   b) brain   c) heart

5) It's not surprising that Nicole gets such good grades. She's as _____ as a tack.

   a) smart   b) sharp   c) clever

6) When Peter _____ his temper, it's very scary. He throws furniture everywhere.

   a) loses   b) finds   c) opens

7) After Jane started hitting the _____, her grades started improving immediately.

   a) work   b) books   c) teachers

8) Nicole said something _____ her breath, but I couldn't hear it. When I asked her to repeat it, she refused.

   a) on   b) about   c) under

9) Will Ted ever be the best student in his class? Sure, when _____ fly!

   a) sheep   b) goats   c) pigs

10) A positive attitude leads to success. When things get difficult, it's important to keep your _____ up.

   a) chin   b) neck   c) head

11) Bob was all stressed _____ because the traffic was making him late for a doctor's appointment.

   a) over   b) out   c) up

12) Frank knew that the judge had already decided he was guilty. There was no point _____ arguing with him.

   a) in   b) around   c) about

13) Some people think Nicole and Susan are sisters. That really _____ Nicole crazy!

   a) does   b) causes   c) drives

14) Ted has been slacking _____ since the first day of high school, so it's not surprising that he's doing so poorly.

   a) around   b) off   c) about

15) During the Depression in the 1930's, many families in America were living from hand to _____.

   a) arm   b) mouth   c) hand

CROSSWORD PUZZLE

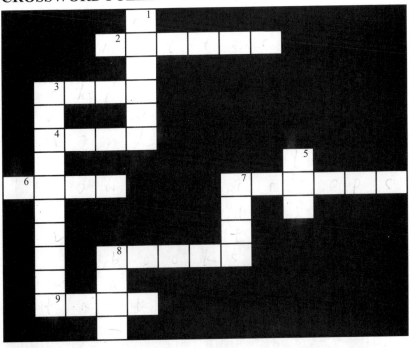

ANSWERS TO REVIEW, p. 161

Across

2. "What's the _____?" Sue asked Bob. "You look very unhappy."
3. Sue doesn't want Bob to be sad. She wants him to keep his _____ up.
4. Bob's boss doesn't want Bob back. He's already made up his _____.
6. After failing his chemistry class once, Ted is taking it again. "Don't _____ it this time!" said his father.
7. Bob doesn't like the people at Honest Abe's Furniture Store. They give him the _____.
8. Ted's father wants him to study more. He tells Ted to hit the _____.
9. You got an "A" in every subject? That's very impressive! You must be as sharp as a _____.

Down

1. Bob was _____. Now he needs to find a new job.
3. Nicole's teacher was pleased with her and paid her a _____.
5. Ted's fancy new CD player cost an arm and a _____.
7. Ted is doing poorly in chemistry because he _____ class so often.
8. I wouldn't trust Lisa. She has a long history of stabbing her friends in the _____.

39

SUSAN STAYS HOME AND BAKES COOKIES

Susan decides to cheer up her husband. Bob loves her homemade cookies. Nicole suggests she start a cookie business.

Susan: Bob, I baked cookies for you.

Bob: That was so nice of you, dear. You've got a **heart of gold**!

Susan: Go ahead and **pig out**!

Bob: These are delicious!

Susan: I thought they might **cheer you up**. You've been **in a bad mood** lately.

Bob: I guess I have been a little **on edge**. But these cookies are **just what the doctor ordered**!

Nicole: Do I smell cookies?

Susan: Yes, Nicole. **Help yourself**.

Nicole: Yum-yum.* These are **out of this world**. You could **go into business** selling these!

Bob: You could call them Susan's Scrumptious Cookies. You'd **make a bundle**.

Susan: **Good thinking!**

Nicole: Don't forget to **give me credit** for the idea after you're rich and famous!

Susan: You know I always **give credit where credit is due**!

* Yum-yum: this is said when something is delicious. You can also say "mmm, mmm" or "mmm-mmm, good."

IDIOMS – LESSON 6

(to) cheer someone up – to make someone happy

EXAMPLE 1: Susan called her friend in the hospital to **cheer her up**.
EXAMPLE 2: My father has been depressed for weeks now. I don't know what to do to **cheer him up**.
NOTE: You can tell somebody to "Cheer up!" if they are feeling sad.

(to) give (someone) credit – to acknowledge someone's contribution; to recognize a positive trait in someone

EXAMPLE 1: The scientist **gave his assistant credit** for the discovery.
EXAMPLE 2: I can't believe you asked your boss for a raise when your company is doing so poorly. I must **give you credit** for your courage!

(to) give credit where credit is due – to give thanks or acknowledgement to the person who deserves it

EXAMPLE: I will be sure to thank you when I give my speech. I always **give credit where credit is due**.

(to) go into business – to start a business

EXAMPLE 1: Jeff decided to **go into business** selling baseball cards.
EXAMPLE 2: Eva **went into business** selling her homemade muffins.

good thinking – good idea; smart planning

EXAMPLE 1: I'm glad you brought an umbrella — that was **good thinking**!
EXAMPLE 2: You reserved our movie tickets over the Internet? **Good thinking**!

(to) have a heart of gold – to be very kind and giving

EXAMPLE 1: Alexander **has a heart of gold** and always thinks of others before himself.
EXAMPLE 2: You adopted five children from a Romanian orphanage? You've got a **heart of gold**!

Help yourself – serve yourself

EXAMPLE 1: "**Help yourselves** to cookies and coffee," said Maria before the meeting started.
EXAMPLE 2: You don't need to wait for me to offer you something. Please just **help yourself** to whatever you want.

NOTE: Pay attention to the reflexive form: Help *yourself* in singular, help *yourselves* in plural.

(to be) in a bad mood – unhappy; depressed; irritable

EXAMPLE 1: After her boyfriend broke up with her, Nicole was **in a bad mood** for several days.
EXAMPLE 2: I don't like to see you **in a bad mood**. How can I cheer you up?

just what the doctor ordered – exactly what was needed

EXAMPLE 1: Martin wanted a hot drink after spending the day skiing. A cup of hot cocoa was **just what the doctor ordered**.
EXAMPLE 2: Our trip to Florida was so relaxing. It was **just what the doctor ordered**!

(to) make a bundle – to make a lot of money

EXAMPLE 1: Bob's friend Charles **made a bundle** in the stock market and retired at age 45.
EXAMPLE 2: Sara **made a bundle** selling her old fur coats on eBay, a website where you can buy and sell used things.

(to be) on edge – nervous; irritable

EXAMPLE 1: Whenever Susan feels **on edge**, she takes several deep breaths and starts to feel more relaxed.
EXAMPLE 2: Ever since his car accident, Neil has felt **on edge**.

out of this world – delicious

EXAMPLE 1: Mrs. Field's oatmeal raisin cookies are **out of this world**!
EXAMPLE 2: Mmmm, I love your chicken soup. It's **out of this world**!

(to) pig out [slang] – to eat greedily; to stuff oneself

EXAMPLE 1: Ted **pigged out** on hot dogs and hamburgers at the barbeque and then got a stomachache.
EXAMPLE 2: "Nicole, stop **pigging out** on cookies or you'll never be able to eat your dinner!"

NOTE: Pay attention to the preposition "on" after the verb "to pig out." One can **pig out on** hotdogs, **pig out on** candy, **pig out on** ice cream.

Choose the best substitute for the phrase or sentence in bold:

1) Thanks for baking cookies for me. **You've got a heart of gold**.
   a) You're a very nice person.
   b) You're a reliable person.
   c) You're very generous with your money.

2) I baked these cookies for you. **Why don't you pig out?**
   a) Please take just one cookie.
   b) Take as many cookies as you like.
   c) Why don't you ever eat my cookies?

3) I know you'll like my cookies since **you've got a sweet tooth**.
   a) your teeth are hurting
   b) you don't like sweet things
   c) you like sweet things

4) **You should go into business selling cookies**.
   a) You should go to the store and buy some cookies.
   b) You should try to get a job baking cookies.
   c) You should start a company that sells cookies.

5) I baked these cookies. **Help yourself!**
   a) Let me get you one!
   b) Take some!
   c) You need to get some help!

6) If you went into business selling these delicious cookies, **you'd make a bundle**.
   a) you'd make many cookies
   b) you'd make a lot of money
   c) you'd make a few dollars

7) **Good thinking!**
   a) That's a good idea!
   b) It's good that you're thinking!
   c) Keep thinking good thoughts!

8) I was thirsty. This iced tea is **just what the doctor ordered.**
   a) exactly what I needed
   b) very healthy for me
   c) exactly what my doctor recommended

ANSWERS TO LESSON 6, p. 161

SUSAN HIRES BOB TO RUN HER BUSINESS

Susan stays up all night thinking about her cookie business. In the morning, she discusses it with Bob. Bob agrees to work for her.

Bob: You're up **bright and early** this morning, Susan.

Susan: I **didn't sleep a wink**. I was awake all night thinking about the new business.

Bob: Running your own business is lots of work. Are you prepared to **work like a dog**?

Susan: No. But I am prepared to hire *you* to run the business.

Bob: You want *me* to run a cookie business? **Fat chance!**

Susan: Why not?

Bob: **I don't have a clue** about making cookies. I don't even know how to turn the oven on!

Susan: I'll give you a **crash course**.

Bob: Do I have to do the baking?

Susan: No. You'll just manage the business side.

Bob: **Needless to say**, I have **mixed feelings** about working for you.

Susan: I'll be nice. I promise you'll be a **happy camper**.

Bob: Okay. **Let's give it a shot**, boss!

IDIOMS – LESSON 7

bright and early – early in the morning

EXAMPLE 1: Our flight to Berlin leaves at 7:00 a.m. tomorrow, so we'll have to get up **bright and early**.
EXAMPLE 2: We have lots of cookies to bake so we'll have to start **bright and early** tomorrow.

SYNONYM: at the crack of dawn

crash course – short and intensive instruction

EXAMPLE 1: Yesterday, Joan's son sat down with her for a couple of hours and gave her a **crash course** on using the Internet.
EXAMPLE 2: Rachel had a date on Friday night with an auto mechanic. He gave her a **crash course** on changing her oil.

Fat chance! – definitely not

EXAMPLE 1: The boys at school are always laughing at Dana. Will she be invited to the school dance? **Fat chance!**
EXAMPLE 2: You want to borrow my new car and drive it across the country? **Fat chance!**

SYNONYMS: never in a million years; no way!

(to) give it a shot – to try something

EXAMPLE 1: I've never tried to make wine in my bathtub before, but perhaps I'll **give it a shot**.
EXAMPLE 2: You can't open that jar? Let me **give it a shot**.

SYNONYMS: to give it a try; to try one's hand at something

NOTE: "To give it one's best shot" means to try as hard as one can. I know you're nervous about the interview — just **give it your best shot**.

happy camper [slang] – a happy person; a satisfied participant

EXAMPLE 1: When Linda's passport was stolen in Florence, she was not a **happy camper**.

EXAMPLE 2: Steve is taking five difficult courses this semester. He's not a **happy camper**!

NOTE: This expression is usually used in the negative (<u>not</u> a happy camper).

(to have) mixed feelings – to feel positive about one aspect of something and negative about another

EXAMPLE 1: When our houseguests decided to stay for another week, I had **mixed feelings**. On the one hand, I enjoyed hanging out with them. On the other hand, I was tired of cooking for them.

EXAMPLE 2: I have **mixed feelings** about the president of our company. He's good with the clients, but he's nasty to his employees.

needless to say – obviously

EXAMPLE 1: You've got a test tomorrow morning. **Needless to say**, you can't stay out late tonight.

EXAMPLE 2: **Needless to say**, you shouldn't have waited until Christmas Eve to do your shopping. The stores are going to be very crowded!

SYNONYM: it goes without saying. Example: You've got a test tomorrow, so **it goes without saying** that you can't stay out late tonight.

(to) not have a clue – to know nothing about

EXAMPLE 1: Bob talks about working at McDonald's, but the truth is he **doesn't have a clue** about making hamburgers.

EXAMPLE 2: "Do you know how to fix a broken printer?" – "No, I **don't have a clue**!"

(to) not sleep a wink – to be awake all night

EXAMPLE 1: Ted was so nervous about his chemistry test that he didn't **sleep a wink** the night before.

EXAMPLE 2: It's not surprising that Jill **didn't sleep a wink** last night. She drank a large cup of coffee before going to bed.

(to) work like a dog – to work very hard

EXAMPLE 1: Larry became an investment banker after college, and now he **works like a dog**.

EXAMPLE 2: Al **worked like a dog** on his term paper and got an "A+" on it.

SYNONYMS: to work one's tail off; to work like a horse; to work one's fingers to the bone

✎ PRACTICE THE IDIOMS

Fill in the blank with the missing word:

1) Bob was surprised to see his wife up ____ and early in the morning.

    a) light   b) bright   c) ready

2) Last week I worked 80 hours. I really worked like a ____.

    a) dog   b) cat   c) squirrel

3) Bob had never baked anything before in his life. He didn't even have a ____ about how to turn the oven on.

    a) hint   b) suggestion   c) clue

4) If you need to learn something quickly, you'd better take a ____ course.

    a) crash   b) fast   c) beginner's

5) Bob wasn't sure he wanted to work for his wife. He had ____ feelings.

    a) nervous   b) mixed   c) confused

6) Jennifer's boss is lousy and her salary is low. She's not a happy ____.

    a) scout   b) tourist   c) camper

7) Bob decided to work for Susan. He figured he'd give it a ____.

    a) shot   b) pop   c) choice

8) Nicole was up all night finishing her Spanish homework. She didn't sleep a ____.

    a) drink   b) blink   c) wink

ANSWERS TO LESSON 7, p. 161

TED FORMS A ROCK BAND

Ted plans to become a successful musician. First, he needs Susan to loan him money for a new guitar. Susan suggests that Ted bake cookies to earn the money.

Susan: You're **in good spirits** today, Ted.

Ted: I've got great news, Mom.

Susan: What is it?

Ted: Amber and I are going to start a rock band!

Susan: **Good for you!**

Ted: Mom, I'm not going to **beat around the bush**. I need to borrow $1,000 for a new guitar.

Susan: Ted, your father and I can't **shell out** that much. We aren't **made of money**.

Ted: You're not? I thought you were millionaires, like Donald and Ivana Trump!*

Susan: Ha ha. This is no time to be a **wise guy**!

Ted: I promise I'll pay you back.

Susan: How?

51

Ted: We're going to **take the music world by storm** and make lots of money.

Susan: That sounds like a **pipe dream**. Aren't high school rock bands a **dime a dozen**?

Ted: Yeah, but we're different. With my guitar playing and Amber's beautiful voice, we're sure to **make a splash**!

Susan: Well, we're going through **hard times**. You're going to have to work for that $1,000.

Ted: How?

Susan: You can bake cookies.

Ted: I bet Mrs. Clapton never made Eric** bake cookies, but I guess **those are the breaks**.

* Donald Trump is a famous American millionaire who made his money in real estate. Ivana is his ex-wife.

** Eric Clapton is a very popular guitarist.

IDIOMS – LESSON 8

(to) beat around the bush – to talk *around* the subject; to avoid getting to the point

EXAMPLE 1: Kara **beat around the bush** for an hour, then finally told us she needed a ride to Kennedy Airport.
EXAMPLE 2: If you want something, tell me. Don't **beat around the bush**!

dime a dozen – so plentiful as to be nothing special; common

EXAMPLE 1: Reality TV shows are a **dime a dozen** these days.
EXAMPLE 2: There are so many Starbucks coffee shops in Manhattan, they're a **dime a dozen**.

NOTE: This expression comes from the fact that a "dime" is worth only ten cents (very little value).

Good for you! – Good job! Well done!

EXAMPLE 1: You won $100,000 on the TV game show *Jeopardy*? **Good for you!**

EXAMPLE 2: You passed your math test? **Good for you!**

hard times – a time of difficulty

EXAMPLE 1: Since his wife left him for her dentist, Dan has been going through **hard times.**

EXAMPLE 2: Nancy's family is going through **hard times.** Her father just lost his job.

(to be) in good spirits – happy; in a good mood

EXAMPLE 1: After she won the tennis tournament, Elizabeth was **in good spirits.**

EXAMPLE 2: Sam was **in good spirits** after receiving his Christmas bonus.

made of money – very rich

EXAMPLE 1: My neighbor is re-modeling his house to look like Versailles. He doesn't have good taste, but he certainly is **made of money.**

EXAMPLE 2: Max should be willing to loan you $10,000 to start your new business. He's **made of money.**

SYNONYMS: loaded; rolling in dough; to have money to burn

(to) make a splash – to win popularity quickly

EXAMPLE 1: Nicole's beautiful cousin Cecilia from Santo Domingo really **made a splash** at the high school dance.

EXAMPLE 2: Those new jeans really **made a splash.** All the kids are wearing them.

SYNONYM: to be a hit

(to) pay (someone) back – to repay a loan or debt

EXAMPLE 1: Nicole **paid her friend back** the $10 she borrowed.

EXAMPLE 2: You can borrow $50, but don't forget to **pay me back!**

NOTE: "Pay back" also means to "get revenge." Example: I know you're the one who stole my car, and one day I'll think of a way to **pay you back!**

pipe dream – an unrealistic hope

EXAMPLE 1: Susan would like to move to New Zealand and write romance novels, but she knows that's just a **pipe dream.**

EXAMPLE 2: You want to become a famous actor on Broadway? That sounds like a **pipe dream.**

(to) shell out – to pay (often more than one would like)

EXAMPLE 1: Bob **shelled out** $5,000 for Nicole's piano lessons before she decided she'd rather play the flute.
EXAMPLE 2: How much am I going to have to **shell out** to get two tickets to the Rolling Stones concert?

(to) take (something) by storm – to win popularity quickly

EXAMPLE 1: The play "The Producers" really **took New York by storm**.
EXAMPLE 2: That new restaurant really **took Chicago by storm**!

(that's *or* those are) the breaks – when something bad happens and you can't do anything about it

EXAMPLE 1: By the time we got to the theater, the new Harry Potter movie was already sold out. Oh well, **that's the breaks**!
EXAMPLE 2: Your glasses fell on a rock and broke while you were fishing? **Those are the breaks**!

wise guy [slang] – a smart aleck; one who makes a lot of sarcastic comments

EXAMPLE 1: When Mrs. Lee asked Joey what he wanted to be when he grew up, he said, "An adult." She told him not to be such a **wise guy**.
EXAMPLE 2: That clerk in the video store is a real **wise guy**. He's always making nasty comments about the customers.

SYNONYMS: wise ass [rude], smart ass [rude]

✎ PRACTICE THE IDIOMS

Choose the best substitute for the phrase in bold:

1) I'm **in good spirits** today because I got a promotion at work.
   a) happy
   b) drunk
   c) tired

2) Renting an apartment on Park Avenue in Manhattan is difficult, unless you're **made of money**.
   a) wealthy
   b) strange
   c) famous

3) My friend's daughter paints beautiful pictures. In a few years, **she'll take the art world by storm**.
   a) something bad will happen and she'll lose her job
   b) she'll draw an excellent painting of a storm
   c) she'll become a very successful artist

4) Susan thinks that Ted's plan to become a famous rock star is **a pipe dream**.
   a) something that is not likely to happen
   b) Ted's biggest hope
   c) something very realistic

5) If you're looking for a new suit, you shouldn't have a problem. Clothing shops in this town are **a dime a dozen**.
   a) hard to find
   b) everywhere
   c) lousy

6) Ted performed at his high school dance. He knew he'd **made a splash** when all the girls started singing along.
   a) done something wrong
   b) made a very positive impression
   c) created waves

7) Being **a wise guy** can be fun, but it might not make you popular with your teachers.
   a) a very intelligent person
   b) an obnoxious person who makes sarcastic comments
   c) a person whom everybody admires

8) Nicole wants to attend Yale, but her parents don't want to **shell out** $100,000 for the tuition.
   a) waste
   b) save
   c) pay

ANSWERS TO LESSON 8, p. 161

LESSON 9

NICOLE FOR PRESIDENT!

Nicole discusses her plans to run for student body president. Nicole wants Ted to ask his friends to vote for her. Ted agrees, in exchange for Nicole's help with his homework.

Nicole: I've decided to run for student body president! If I'm going to become a senator one day, I should **get some experience under my belt** now.

Ted: Andrea Jenkins is also running. She'll give you a **run for your money**!

Nicole: Andrea Jenkins is an idiot. I'm **by far** the better candidate.

Ted: Don't be so **full of yourself**! I might vote for Andrea.

Nicole: Stop **kidding around. Let's get down to business**. I need your help.

Ted: You want *me* to help *you*?

Nicole: Yes. I need you to **talk** your friends **into** voting for me.

Ted: But you never **give my friends the time of day**. All you give them is the **cold shoulder**.

Nicole: That's because they've got blue hair and nose rings!

Ted: They're better than your friends — a bunch of **goody-goodies** and **brown-nosers**!

Nicole: That's **beside the point**. Let's talk about *your* friends and *their* votes.

Ted: Okay. **You scratch my back and I'll scratch yours**. If you do my chemistry homework, I'll help you get the votes.

Nicole: I'm not **crazy about** that idea. But, okay, **it's a deal**. I hope I can **count on you**.

IDIOMS – LESSON 9

beside the point – *see Lesson 3*

brown-noser [slang] – a person who's constantly trying to win favor with people above them, such as teachers or bosses

EXAMPLE 1: Lauren is such a **brown-noser**. She's always telling her teacher how much she enjoys class.
EXAMPLE 2: Dennis brought the boss lunch today? What a **brown-noser**!

NOTE: You will also see the verb form of this expression: "to brown-nose." Example: Dennis is always **brown-nosing** the boss, but I still don't think he's going to get a promotion.

by far – by a wide margin; by a great difference

EXAMPLE 1: Some people think Tom Hanks is **by far** the best actor in America today.
EXAMPLE 2: Mediterranean Grill is **by far** the best restaurant in town. No wonder it's so hard to get a reservation there!

SYNONYMS: by a long shot; far and away; hands down

(to) count on someone – to depend or rely on someone

EXAMPLE 1: My brother has a great sense of humor, so I can always **count on him** to cheer me up.

EXAMPLE 2: If I can **count on you** to wake me up, I won't set my alarm clock.

(to be) crazy about – *see Lesson 3*

full of oneself – to think too much of oneself

EXAMPLE 1: After Angela appeared on the cover of *Vogue* magazine, she was really **full of herself**.

EXAMPLE 2: Mitch thinks he's really great. He's so **full of himself**.

(to) get down to business – to get serious about a task

EXAMPLE 1: The book club members spent the first two hours of their meeting eating and drinking before finally **getting down to business**.

EXAMPLE 2: Our dinner guests are arriving in two hours. We'd better **get down to business** and start preparing.

(to) get *or* to have under one's belt – to have or to get experience

EXAMPLE 1: Kristen had three years of working for a large law firm **under her belt** before leaving to start her own firm.

EXAMPLE 2: Ernie needs to get an MBA **under his belt** to get the job he wants.

(to) give (someone) a run for (one's) money – to be strong competition

EXAMPLE 1: We lost the soccer tournament, but we certainly **gave the girls from Stamford High School a run for their money**.

EXAMPLE 2: Tina is a good tennis player and always **gives me a run for my money**.

(to) give someone the cold shoulder – to be cold to someone on purpose; to snub someone

EXAMPLE 1: When Lisa saw Amber at the mall, she didn't even stop to talk to her. She really **gave her the cold shoulder**.

EXAMPLE 2: I can't understand why Joe would **give you the cold shoulder**. I thought you two were good friends!

SYNONYM: to blow someone off. Example: Amber can't understand why Lisa **blew her off** at the mall.

(to not) give someone the time of day – to ignore someone; to refuse to pay any attention to someone

EXAMPLE 1: Sandra never **gave me the time of day** back in college, but now she calls me all the time for advice.

EXAMPLE 2: Why don't you find a new stockbroker? Yours is always so busy, she barely **gives you the time of day**.

goody-goody – self-righteously or smugly good

EXAMPLE 1: **Goody-goodies** usually sit in the front row and smile at the teacher during class.

EXAMPLE 2: Samantha is a real **goody-goody**. She always offers to erase the blackboard at the end of class.

SYNONYMS: goody two-shoes; teacher's pet

it's a deal – I agree (to a proposal or offer)

EXAMPLE 1: You'll make dinner every night for a month if I help you with your homework? Okay, **it's a deal**!

EXAMPLE 2: "If you rake up all the leaves in front of the house, I'll do the dishes." – "**It's a deal!**"

(to) kid around – to joke around; to tease

EXAMPLE 1: Jeremy loves to **kid around**, so don't be offended by anything he says.

EXAMPLE 2: While they were **kidding around**, Tim accidentally poked Rob in the eye. He had to be rushed to the emergency room of the hospital.

NOTE: You will often here this in the negative "not kidding around." This means to take something very seriously. Example: The White House is **not kidding around** with airport security.

(to) talk into – to persuade; to convince

EXAMPLE 1: Chris didn't want to jump out of the plane, but Erin **talked him into it**.

EXAMPLE 2: Stop trying to **talk me into** going to the dance club on Saturday night. I already decided that I'm going to Maria's party instead.

you scratch my back and I'll scratch yours – if you do me a favor, I'll do you a favor; let's cooperate

EXAMPLE 1: I'll help you with your homework if you do the dishes. **You scratch my back and I'll scratch yours**.

EXAMPLE 2: If I drive you into the city, will you pick up my dry cleaning? **You scratch my back and I'll scratch yours**.

✎ Practice the Idioms

Fill in the blank with the missing word:

1) Nicole is very reliable. You can always count _____ her.

   a) in   b) on   c) with

2) I need to ask you for your help, and I'll do something nice for you in return. You scratch my _____ and I'll scratch yours.

   a) back   b) neck   c) foot

3) Stop kidding _____! Tell me where you hid my shoes.

   a) about   b) around   c) into

4) I can't believe that Lisa gave you the _____ shoulder. I thought you two were friends.

   a) hot   b) freezing   c) cold

5) Ted's friends didn't want to vote for Nicole, but Ted talked them _____ it.

   a) into   b) around   c) for

6) Although Jim Greene was _____ far the more qualified candidate, he lost the election because of a scandal.

   a) way   b) in   c) by

7) Denise is really full _____ herself. She thinks she's the smartest and most beautiful woman in the world.

   a) with   b) of   c) in

8) Nicole thinks that Andrea is a snob. She says Andrea won't _____ her the time of day.

   a) give   b) allow   c) tell

ANSWERS TO LESSON 9, p. 162

BOB VISITS THE VILLAGE MARKET

Bob goes to the Village Market, a supermarket in town. He asks Carol, the owner of the store, if she would like to sell Susan's Scrumptious Cookies. Carol agrees, but isn't able to tell Bob how much she'll pay him.

Bob: Thank you for **making time for** me today, Carol.

Carol: **Don't mention it,** Bob. **What's up**?

Bob: My wife baked these cookies **from scratch**. Please take one.

Carol: Mmmm, chewy. These are **out of this world**!

Bob: My wife's a great cook.

Carol: **You can say that again**. I don't want to **make a pig of** myself, but let me take a few more.

Bob: *Oink oink!* **Just kidding!**

Carol: I'd like to sell these at the Village Market. My customers will **go nuts** over these!

Bob: How much would you pay us for each cookie?

Carol: I'm not sure. I need to **roll up my sleeves** and **figure out** the finances.

Bob: Can you give me a **ballpark figure** now?

Carol: I don't want to **jump the gun**. **Sit tight** for now, and we'll **talk things over** this evening.

IDIOMS – LESSON 10

ballpark figure – an approximate number

EXAMPLE 1: The auto mechanic didn't know exactly how much the repairs would cost, but he was able to give me a **ballpark figure**.
EXAMPLE 2: The plumber estimated that it would cost $150 to fix our sink, but that was just a **ballpark figure**.

Don't mention it! – you're welcome

EXAMPLE 1: "Thanks for bringing the cookies," I said to Susan. "**Don't mention it!**" she replied.
EXAMPLE 2: "Thanks for picking up my suit at the dry cleaners." – "**Don't mention it**. It was my pleasure."

(to) figure out – to solve; to determine

EXAMPLE 1: Ted couldn't **figure out** one of his math problems, so he asked his sister for help.
EXAMPLE 2: Susan is sure she'll never **figure out** why kids today behave the way they do.

from scratch – from the beginning; using all fresh ingredients rather than using a prepared mix

EXAMPLE 1: The house was in such bad shape, they decided to tear it down and re-build it **from scratch**.
EXAMPLE 2: You baked these muffins **from scratch**? They're delicious!

(to) go nuts [slang] – to react with great enthusiasm

EXAMPLE 1: When Tiger Woods got a hole-in-one during the golf tournament, the crowd **went nuts**.
EXAMPLE 2: When Eminem appeared on stage, everybody **went nuts**.

NOTE: This expression also means "to go crazy" or "to become crazy with anger." Example: Jim **went nuts** when his wife told him she was leaving him for another man.

(to) jump the gun – to start doing something too soon or ahead of everybody else

EXAMPLE 1: Nicole really **jumped the gun** by writing her acceptance speech before the results of the elections were announced.
EXAMPLE 2: The bookstore **jumped the gun** by selling the new Harry Potter book two weeks before its official release date.

just kidding – talking more to get a laugh than anything

EXAMPLE 1: I was **just kidding** when I said your new orange dress makes you look like a pumpkin.
EXAMPLE 2: Are you sure that's your boyfriend? I thought he was your grandfather. **Just kidding**!

(to) make a pig of oneself [slang] – to overeat; to eat too much

EXAMPLE 1: I **made a pig of myself** by eating four slices of pie.
EXAMPLE 2: Of course you could eat another hamburger, but you don't want to **make a pig of yourself**.

(to) make time for – to put time in one's schedule for something

EXAMPLE 1: Don is a busy lawyer, but he always **makes time for** his family.
EXAMPLE 2: I'll be sure to **make time for** you when you visit me.

out of this world – *see Lesson 6*

(to) roll up one's sleeves – to prepare to work

EXAMPLE 1: Let's **roll up our sleeves** and finish making these cookies!
EXAMPLE 2: You'd better **roll up your sleeves** and finish your homework.

(to) sit tight – to wait patiently

EXAMPLE 1: Nicole won't hear back from the colleges she applied to until April. For now, she'll just have to **sit tight**.
EXAMPLE 2: **Sit tight**, the doctor will be with you in a few minutes.

(to) talk over – *see Lesson 1*

What's up? – What's going on? What's new?

EXAMPLE 1: **What's up?** I haven't spoken to you in a long time.
EXAMPLE 2: You never call me anymore. **What's up** with that?

you can say that again – I agree with you

EXAMPLE 1: You think our house needs repairs? **You can say that again** — even our toilet is broken!
EXAMPLE 2: "The weather is so nasty today." – "**You can say that again**! I don't even want to go outside!"

✎ PRACTICE THE IDIOMS

Imagine that you are Bob and that you're meeting with Carol from the Village Market to sell her your cookies. Choose the most appropriate replies to Carol's questions and statements:

1) *Carol:* "I'm glad I was able to make time to see you today."
   Bob's reply:
   a) "I guess I'll see you tomorrow then."
   b) "It must be nice to have so much free time."
   c) "Yes, thanks for fitting me into your busy schedule."

2) *Carol:* "What's up?"
   Bob's reply:
   a) "Fine, thank you."
   b) "I'd like to discuss a business deal with you."
   c) "I don't know. Let me check with my wife."

3) *Carol:* "These cookies are out of this world. What do you think?"
   Bob's reply:
   a) "I agree. They're delicious!"
   b) "I don't know where they are."
   c) "No thanks. I've already had ten cookies."

4) *Carol:* "Did your wife make these from scratch?"
   Bob's reply:
   a) "No, she made them from flour, eggs, and sugar."
   b) "Yes, she did. She loves to bake."
   c) "Yes. She bought a roll of Pillsbury frozen dough and heated it in the oven for 15 minutes."

5) *Carol:* "I ate seven cookies. Do you think I've made a pig of myself?"
   Bob's reply:
   a) "Not at all. These cookies are hard to resist!"
   b) "Yes. You look just like a pig."
   c) "Yes. Pigs love to eat cookies too."

6) *Carol:* "I think my customers will go nuts over these cookies."
   Bob's reply:
       a) "I agree. After all, they're very good!"
       b) "Nuts? Sure, we can put nuts in the cookies."
       c) "I disagree. They'll probably like them."

7) *Carol:* "Bob, I'm not ready to give you a ballpark figure yet."
   Bob's reply:
       a) "Okay, how about one dollar per cookie?"
       b) "When you're ready, we can sell them in the ballpark."
       c) "Okay, I can wait until tomorrow."

8) *Carol:* "I don't want to jump the gun by discussing details now."
   Bob's reply:
       a) "I understand. Take some time to think about it."
       b) "I didn't say anything about selling you guns."
       c) "Thanks, I'd love an answer right now."

ANSWERS TO LESSON 10, p. 162

 Review for Lessons 6-10

Choose the best substitute for the phrase in bold:

1) This apple pie is **out of this world**.
       a) not bad
       b) from another planet
       c) delicious

2) Jane was feeling **on edge**, so she went to a day spa to relax.
       a) anxious
       b) relaxed
       c) angry

3) You ate 15 cookies? You really **made a pig of yourself**!
       a) turned into an animal with a snout and tail
       b) made yourself sick
       c) ate more than you should have

4) Bob wasn't sure he wanted to work for his wife's cookie company, but she **talked him into it**.
   a) forced him
   b) convinced him
   c) asked him

5) Nancy **doesn't have a clue** about the Internet. She's never even used e-mail.
   a) understands deeply
   b) knows nothing
   c) is learning a lot

6) Stop **beating around the bush**! I don't know what you're trying to tell me.
   a) avoiding the subject
   b) hitting the trees
   c) repeating yourself

7) Paul likes to draw silly cartoons of his classmates on the blackboard before class. He's a **wise guy**.
   a) bad student
   b) smart person
   c) sarcastic person

8) Tom needed to learn how to ride a horse before his trip to Ireland, so he took a **crash course.**
   a) short, intensive class
   b) class in falling down
   c) semester-long class

9) Laura **made a bundle** when she was younger, and now she spends every day on the golf course.
   a) had a good job
   b) made lots of money
   c) stole money

10) The doctor will be with you soon. Please **sit tight**.
   a) come back later
   b) wait patiently
   c) follow me

CROSSWORD PUZZLE

Across

2. Stop beating around the ____ and get to the point already!
6. Susan's cookies really made a ____ at the Village Market. Everybody loved them!
7. You want to be a famous painter? That sounds like a ____ dream!
8. When Ted was asked to perform at the high school dance, he was one happy ____ .
11. When I ran into Mary at the mall, she gave me the cold ____.
12. Stop ____ around! We've got work to do.

Down

1. If you need to learn something quickly, you can take a ____ course.
2. I don't need an exact number right now. A ____ figure is fine.
3. I always prefer cakes and cookies made from ____.
4. If there's one thing teachers hate, it's a ____ guy.
5. It's nice when a boss gives you the ____ for your ideas.
9. I have ____ feelings about visiting Puerto Rico in August. On the one hand, it won't be too full of tourists. On the other hand, it will be very hot.
10. Susan is always helping others. She's got a heart of ____.
13. I don't know how I got talked ____ taking a tour of Costa Rica during the rainy season.

ANSWERS TO REVIEW, p. 162

BOB DRIVES A HARD BARGAIN

Carol from the Village Market calls Bob to discuss Susan's Scrumptious Cookies. Carol and Bob discuss how much Bob will receive for each cookie.

Carol: Hi Bob. **How's it going**?

Bob: Fine thanks, Carol. How are you?

Carol: **Can't complain**. Bob, I've had a chance to **crunch some numbers**. I can pay you 50¢ per cookie.

Bob: That's **out of the question**. At that price, it's not **worth our while**. The ingredients alone cost us 30¢ per cookie.

Carol: Okay, let me **sweeten the deal** — 60¢ per cookie?

Bob: Carol, my wife and I need to **make a living** from this business.

Carol: Okay, okay, you've **twisted my arm**. I'll pay you 75¢ per cookie. **Take it or leave it!**

Bob: **Now you're talking**! We'll take it.

Carol: You **drive a hard bargain**, Bob.

Bob: Yes, but we make a good cookie.

Carol: Let's **get the ball rolling**. Bring me 2,000 cookies on Monday morning by 9 a.m.

IDIOMS – LESSON 11

can't complain – things are going well; I'm fine

EXAMPLE 1: "How's business, Mike?" – "**Can't complain**. I sold a lot of computers this month."
EXAMPLE 2: "How are things going at your new job?" – "**Can't complain**."

(to) crunch numbers – to perform calculations (especially financial calculations)

EXAMPLE 1: Scott loves to **crunch numbers**, so he decided to become an accountant.
EXAMPLE 2: Wendy spends all her time at work in front of the computer **crunching numbers** and analyzing sales data.

(to) drive a hard bargain – to be tough in negotiating an agreement; to negotiate something in one's favor

EXAMPLE 1: I wanted to pay less for the car, but the salesman **drove a hard bargain**.
EXAMPLE 2: Eric **drove a hard bargain** and got the company to raise their salary offer by $15,000.

(to) get the ball rolling – to get started

EXAMPLE 1: Let's **get the ball rolling** on this project. We've only got one week to finish it.
EXAMPLE 2: If we don't **get the ball rolling** on our vacation plans soon, we'll end up going nowhere.

How's it going? – How are you?

EXAMPLE 1: "**How's it going**?" I asked Ted. "Everything's fine. How are you?" he replied.
EXAMPLE 2: "**How's it going**?" Vladimir asked me. "Not bad," I replied.

(to) make a living – to earn enough money to support oneself

EXAMPLE 1: Many people laugh at him, but Bill actually **makes a living** selling gourmet dog food.

EXAMPLE 2: Danny makes some money playing his guitar on street corners, but not enough to **make a living**.

now you're talking – you're saying the right thing

EXAMPLE 1: You want to offer me free tickets to the J. Lo concert? **Now you're talking!**

EXAMPLE 2: You'd like to offer me a $10,000 raise and a corner office? **Now you're talking!**

out of the question – impossible

EXAMPLE 1: My friend Emily wanted me to climb Mount McKinley with her, but I told her it was **out of the question**.

EXAMPLE 2: You want to borrow my new car and drive it across the country? I'm sorry, but that's **out of the question**.

(to) sweeten the deal – to make an offer more attractive

EXAMPLE 1: IBM offered to **sweeten the deal** by giving John a company car if he agreed to work for them.

EXAMPLE 2: We really want you to take the job here at Magna Corporation, so let us know what we can do to **sweeten the deal**.

take it or leave it – accept or reject an offer, usually a final one

EXAMPLE 1: The highest salary we can offer you is $50,000 a year — **take it or leave it**.

EXAMPLE 2: I'm offering to do the dishes for one week if you'll help me with my science project. **Take it or leave it**.

(to) twist (someone's) arm – to persuade someone; to convince someone

EXAMPLE 1: Ted didn't want to get another tattoo on his back, but Amber **twisted his arm**.

EXAMPLE 2: Okay, you've **twisted my arm**. You can borrow my new car and drive it across the country.

worth one's while – worthy of one's effort or time

EXAMPLE 1: It would be **worth your while** to audition for the game show *Jeopardy*. You'd probably win a lot of money.

EXAMPLE 2: Let me make it **worth your while** to work weekends. I'll pay you an extra $10 per hour on Saturdays and Sundays.

✍ Practice the Idioms

Abe, owner of Honest Abe's Furniture Store, is talking to Jeff about a new advertising campaign for the store. Jeff owns an advertising agency. Complete the dialogue using these idioms:

get the ball rolling	**drive a hard bargain**
crunch some numbers	**how's it going**
out of the question	**now you're talking**
twisted my arm	**make a living**

Abe: Hi, Jeff. _____?

Jeff: Fine, thanks. I've only scheduled a half hour for this meeting, so we'd better _____.

Abe: Jeff, I need you to come up with a new advertising campaign for my furniture shop.

Jeff: I've had a chance to _____, and you'll need to pay me $30,000 to come up with some new ideas.

Abe: Thirty thousand dollars? That's really _____!

Jeff: Listen, Abe, I need to _____ too. I've got a wife and seven children at home.

Abe: I'll pay you $20,000.

Jeff: If you want quality work, you have to pay for it. Let's say $25,000?

Abe: Okay, okay. You've _____. I'll pay you $23,000.

Jeff: _____. That's a fair price.

Abe: You certainly _____.

Jeff: I know, but you'll be happy with my work.

ANSWERS TO LESSON 11, p. 163

74

LESSON 12

BOB'S BIG COOKIE ORDER

The family is gathered around the dinner table. Bob tells them about his deal with the Village Market. He asks his kids for help baking the cookies.

Bob: I know I've been **down in the dumps** since I got fired, but **things are looking up** now. The Village Market wants to sell our cookies.

Nicole: That's great news, Dad!

Bob: We're going to have to bake **like crazy** over the weekend. They want 2,000 cookies by Monday.

Nicole: Two thousand cookies in three days? Don't you think you've **bitten off more than you can chew**?

Ted: Yeah, you're going to be **running around like a chicken with its head cut off**!

Susan: Fortunately, there are four of us here. You kids will have to **pitch in** too.

Nicole: Sorry, but I can't. I have to finish Ted's chemistry homework and then I've got to **get going** on my election speech.

Bob: What's that about doing Ted's chemistry homework?

Ted: **Never mind!** Amber will **help out** with the cookies instead of Nicole.

Susan: **For heaven's sake**, Nicole! It's **like pulling teeth** getting you to do any work around here.

IDIOMS – LESSON 12

(to) bite off more than one can chew – to take on more than one is capable of; to take on too much

EXAMPLE 1: Jennifer is having a dinner party for 50 people, and she can't even cook. I think she's **bitten off more than she can chew**.
EXAMPLE 2: You agreed to host 50 exchange students from Korea? Aren't you afraid you've **bitten off more than you can chew**?

SYNONYM: to be *or* to get in over one's head. Example: Jennifer is in **over her head** with this dinner party!

(to be) down in the dumps – *see Lesson 5*

---

for heaven's sake! – A way of expressing emotions such as surprise, outrage, or impatience

EXAMPLE 1: Hurry up, **for heaven's sake**! You're going to be late for school.
EXAMPLE 2: Oh, **for heaven's sake**! Yesterday, I made three dozen chocolate chip cookies, and today there's only one cookie left!

SYNONYMS: for God's sake, for goodness sake, for Pete's sake

(to) get going – to get started on something; to set off for a destination; to leave

EXAMPLE 1: If you don't **get going** on your homework soon, you're going to be up all night.
EXAMPLE 2: We'd better **get going** to the restaurant now. Otherwise, we'll be late for our seven o'clock reservation.

SYNONYMS: to get a move on; to get the show on the road

(to) help out – to give assistance; to help

EXAMPLE 1: Amber offered to **help out** in the kitchen by chopping nuts.
EXAMPLE 2: I'd be happy to **help out** by baking cookies for the picnic.

SYNONYM: to lend a hand

like a chicken with its head cut off – in a hysterical manner; in a frenzy; in a very nervous way

EXAMPLE 1: Ken was late for work, and he couldn't find his car keys. He was running around his apartment **like a chicken with its head cut off**.
EXAMPLE 2: Patricia ran around the school looking for her lost backpack **like a chicken with its head cut off**.

NOTE: This idiom is usually used with the phrase "to run around" as in the above examples.

like crazy – with great speed or enthusiasm

EXAMPLE 1: When Pete Sampras won the tennis match, the crowd started cheering **like crazy**.
EXAMPLE 2: Ann ran **like crazy**, but she still didn't manage to catch the bus.

like pulling teeth – very difficult

EXAMPLE 1: It's **like pulling teeth** getting Max to talk about his girlfriend.
EXAMPLE 2: Kyle hates to study. It's **like pulling teeth** getting him to do his homework every night.

never mind – don't worry about something; forget it; it doesn't matter

EXAMPLE 1: You forgot to pick up eggs at the supermarket? **Never mind**. I'll get them tomorrow morning.
EXAMPLE 2: **Never mind** what your friends say. You need to do what you think is right.

(to) pitch in – to help

EXAMPLE 1: Nicole offered to **pitch in** and clean up her neighborhood beach. She picked up five plastic cups and an old towel.
EXAMPLE 2: If you need my help, just ask. I'd be happy to **pitch in**.

SYNONYMS: to lend a hand, to lend a helping hand; to help out

(to) run around – to move about quickly

EXAMPLE 1: I've been **running around** all day making final arrangements for our trip to Costa Rica tomorrow.
EXAMPLE 2: Debbie is exhausted. She **ran around** town all day today.

things are looking up – things are improving

EXAMPLE 1: Elizabeth found a wonderful new job and just moved into a beautiful new apartment. **Things are looking up** for her.
EXAMPLE 2: **Things are looking up** with the economy.

✎ PRACTICE THE IDIOMS

Fill in the blank with the missing word:

1) When the sun doesn't shine all winter, it's easy to start feeling down in the _____.

   a) dumps   b) crazy   c) luck

2) Things were so busy at work, I spent the entire week running around like a chicken with its _____ cut off.

   a) beak   b) head   c) neck

3) According to today's newspaper, the economy is improving. Things are looking _____.

   a) up   b) down   c) forward

4) I thought you could help me with my new project. But if you're too busy, never _____. I'll find somebody else.

   a) bother   b) mind   c) worry

5) For heaven's _____! If you don't stop playing those video games, you'll never get your homework done.

   a) angels   b) sake   c) benefit

6) When the school asked Susan to bring cookies to the bake sale, she said she'd be happy to help _____.

   a) in   b) about   c) out

7) When my friend John told me how busy he was preparing for his Halloween party, I offered to pitch _____.

   a) in   b) out   c) him

8) It's like pulling _____ getting Nicole to help out in the kitchen.

   a) hair   b) nails   c) teeth

✪ BONUS PRACTICE

Choose the best substitute for the phrase in bold:

1) Janice is doing all the cooking for her daughter's wedding. I think she's **bitten off more than she can chew**.
   a) accepted too little responsibility
   b) taken too much food into her mouth
   c) taken on more than she can handle

2) If Nicole is going to cover her entire school with election posters, she'd better **get going on** them immediately.
   a) start working on
   b) stop working on
   c) start destroying

3) If you get tired of mowing the lawn, I'd be happy to **help out**.
   a) confuse you
   b) do nothing
   c) assist you

4) Last year, Bill opened a store selling gourmet pet food. This year, he'll open 10 more stores. His business is growing **like crazy!**
   a) very quickly
   b) very slowly
   c) despite being a crazy idea

5) Ever since receiving his rejection letter from Princeton University, Jason has been **down in the dumps**.
   a) happy
   b) sad
   c) encouraged

6) For a long time, Michelle couldn't find a boyfriend. But now **things are looking up**. She met a nice guy last weekend.
   a) her love life is getting even worse
   b) her love life is improving
   c) her love life couldn't get much worse

ANSWERS TO LESSON 12, p. 163

AMBER COMES OVER TO BAKE COOKIES

Ted's girlfriend Amber comes over to help with the cookies. Amber has experience baking cookies from a former job. Susan leaves the kitchen so they can work better.

Ted: Mom, Amber is here to **lend a hand** with the cookies.

Susan: Hi Amber. Nice to see you again.

Amber: Good to see you too, Mrs. Johnson.

Susan: That's an interesting hairstyle.*

Amber: Thanks. I'm glad you think it's cool. Blue hair is **all the rage** this season.

Susan: Well, I'm going to **take a break** now and let you kids **take over**.

Ted: Don't worry, Mom. Your business is **in good hands** with Amber. She really **knows her stuff**.

Amber: That's true. I used to work at Mrs. Field's Cookies** in the mall.

Susan: You don't work there anymore?

Amber: No, I got fired. I have a real **sweet tooth**, and they told me I was eating too many cookies.

Susan: Well, I'm sure you haven't **lost your touch**.

Amber: I might be a bit **out of practice**.

Ted: Mom, you can watch Amber bake if you want. You might **pick up** a few **tricks of the trade**.

Amber: Yes, **feel free**. As a singer, I'm used to performing before an audience!

Susan: Thanks, but I'm going to **get out of the way**. You know what they say: **too many cooks spoil the broth**!

Amber: Will I see you later tonight?

Susan: Yes, I'll be back in a few hours.

Ted: Mom, why don't you just **call it a night** and go to bed. You've been **working your tail off** all day.

* When somebody says something is "interesting" it often means they don't like it, but they want to be polite.

** Mrs. Field's Cookies are gourmet cookies that are sold in malls across the United States.

IDIOMS – LESSON 13

all the rage – the latest fashion; popular right now

EXAMPLE 1: Have you seen those new alligator-skin cowboy boots? They're **all the rage** this season!
EXAMPLE 2: At Nate's high school, salsa dancing is **all the rage** this year.

(to) call it a night – to stop an activity for the rest of the night

EXAMPLE 1: We spent a few hours walking around downtown Chicago. It was so cold that we were ready to **call it a night** by nine o'clock.
EXAMPLE 2: Let's **call it a night** and meet back at the office at seven o'clock tomorrow morning to finish preparing our report.

NOTE: There is also the expression "to call it a day" which means to stop activity for the day.

feel free – go ahead and do something; don't hesitate (to do something)

EXAMPLE 1: "**Feel free** to interrupt me and ask questions during my lecture," said the professor to his students.
EXAMPLE 2: If you need legal advice, **feel free** to call my cousin Fred. He's a lawyer.

(to) get out of the way – to move out of the way; to stop interfering with someone's plans or activities

EXAMPLE 1: If you're not planning on helping us prepare dinner, please **get out of the way**. The kitchen is crowded.
EXAMPLE 2: **Get out of the way!** That truck is backing up and it might run you over.

(to be) in good hands – in good, competent care

EXAMPLE 1: Don't worry — your dog will be **in good hands** while you're on vacation. We'll take her to the New York Dog Spa & Hotel.
EXAMPLE 2: You're **in good hands** with Tony. He's an excellent driver.

(to) know one's stuff – to have an expertise in a field

EXAMPLE 1: Steve has been an auto mechanic for 25 years. He really **knows his stuff**.
EXAMPLE 2: When it comes to cooking, Kristen **knows her stuff**. She spent two years studying at the Culinary Institute of America.

(to) lend a hand – to help

EXAMPLE 1: When Amber saw Susan washing the cookie sheets, she offered to **lend a hand**.
EXAMPLE 2: Would you mind **lending a hand** in the garden? We need to finish planting these flowers before it starts raining.

(to) lose one's touch – to no longer be able to do something well

EXAMPLE 1: I used to make delicious pies, but this one tastes terrible. I think I've **lost my touch**.
EXAMPLE 2: Dr. Stewart used to be a very good doctor, but recently several of his patients have died. He seems to have **lost his touch**!

(to be) out of practice – no longer good at doing something

EXAMPLE 1: Susan studied French in high school, but she hasn't spoken it since. She's really **out of practice**.
EXAMPLE 2: I used to play tennis every day, but I haven't played in years. I'm **out of practice**.

(to) pick up – to acquire; to learn

EXAMPLE 1: Bob **picks up** languages quickly. After two weeks in Spain, he was already speaking Spanish.
EXAMPLE 2: Diana **picked up** some great new ideas at the workshop.

NOTE: "Pick up" has several other meanings, including:
  1) To take from the floor or ground. **Pick up** the pen you dropped.
  2) To buy. I'll **pick up** some burritos on my way home.
  3) To clean up. Let's **pick up** the bedroom before the guests arrive.
  4) To retrieve someone. I'll **pick you up** at seven for our date.

sweet tooth – an enjoyment of sugary foods

EXAMPLE 1: Amber's got a real **sweet tooth**. Last night, she ate a whole box of Godiva chocolates.
EXAMPLE 2: No wonder Liz is so overweight. She's got such a **sweet tooth**!

(to) take a break – to stop and rest from an activity

EXAMPLE 1: Bob always worked 10 hours straight, never **taking a break**.
EXAMPLE 2: Let's **take a break** from our work and go get some ice cream.

(to) take over – to assume control

EXAMPLE 1: After 11 hours of driving, I was getting tired. Fortunately, my friend offered to **take over**.
EXAMPLE 2: My new boss will be **taking over** some of my projects.

too many cooks spoil the broth – too many people involved in an activity can ruin it

EXAMPLE 1: After Bob and Susan edited Nicole's college applications, they were worse than when she started. **Too many cooks spoil the broth**.
EXAMPLE 2: You don't need to help us. We have enough people helping already, and **too many cooks spoil the broth**.

NOTE: Broth is a clear liquid that forms the base for soups.

tricks of the trade – clever shortcuts gained by experience

EXAMPLE 1: The new teacher learned some **tricks of the trade** from Mrs. Blackstone, who'd been teaching at the school for 40 years.
EXAMPLE 2: My new job will be easier once I learn some **tricks of the trade**.

(to) work one's tail off [slang] – to work very hard

EXAMPLE 1: Don **worked his tail off** to save money for his son's education.
EXAMPLE 2: Bob **worked his tail off** at the furniture store, but his boss fired him anyway.

✎ PRACTICE THE IDIOMS

Fill in the blank with the missing word:

1) When Susan was having trouble lifting her heavy mixer, Bob offered to lend a _____ .

   a) finger   b) foot   c) hand

2) Nicole used to play the piano, but she hasn't practiced in five years. She's really _____ practice.

   a) about to   b) into   c) out of

3) You've been working in the kitchen for hours. Why don't you go and _____ a break?

   a) take   b) give   c) do

4) Amber picked up many _____ of the trade while working at Mrs. Field's Cookies in the Stamford Mall.

   a) bits   b) tricks   c) pieces

5) Your shoulder massages are still the best. You haven't _____ your touch.

   a) found   b) lost   c) spoiled

6) After two weeks in Italy, Tom started to pick _____ a few words of Italian, including *cappuccino* and *pizza*.

   a) up   b) out   c) in

7) When Jill got tired of chopping the onions, Jack took _____ .

   a) over   b) off   c) away

8) Whenever we need financial advice, we call Suze Orman. She really knows her _____ .

   a) things   b) stuff   c) matter

ANSWERS TO LESSON 13, p. 163

AMBER AND TED HEAT UP THE KITCHEN

Amber and Ted are in the kitchen baking cookies. Amber asks Ted to give her a kiss, but Ted tells her he's too busy. Then he feels guilty and goes to her. But suddenly, they're not alone!

Amber: Ted, when I met you, it was **love at first sight**.

Ted: I was **nuts about** you from the beginning too, Amber. Don't forget, I **broke up with** that girl Tiffany after I met you.

Amber: Come here and give me a kiss.

Ted: **Give me a break**, Amber! We don't have time for that now. We need to **crank out** these cookies.

Amber: You don't really love me, do you?

Ted: Amber, I'm **head over heels in love with you**. But it's **crunch time** with these cookies.

Amber: Cookies, cookies, cookies — you've got a **one-track mind**. ♫ He loves cookies, yeah, yeah, yeah... ♫

Ted: Amber, I need to keep working, but you can **take a break** if you want.

Amber: No, I'll keep **plugging away**…I'm just your cookie slave. **Go ahead**, **treat me like dirt!**

Ted: Sorry, Amber. Come here and let me give you a quick kiss.

(Susan enters the kitchen)

Susan: Hey, what's going on in here? Are you two making cookies or **making out**?

IDIOMS – LESSON 14

(to) break up with (someone) – to end a relationship with a romantic partner

EXAMPLE 1: When Nicole's boyfriend told her he didn't want to see her anymore, she replied, "I can't believe you're **breaking up with me!**"
EXAMPLE 2: After dating her boyfriend Dan for four years, Erica finally decided to **break up with him**.

(to) crank out – to produce rapidly or in a routine manner

EXAMPLE 1: Last night, Nicole **cranked out** 200 signs for her campaign.
EXAMPLE 2: We just bought a new printer at work. It can **crank out** 20 pages per minute.

crunch time – a short period when there's high pressure to achieve a result

EXAMPLE 1: The entire month of December is **crunch time** for Santa Claus.
EXAMPLE 2: May is **crunch time** for many students. It's when they have their final exams.

Give me a break! – that's ridiculous; that's outrageous

EXAMPLE 1: You want me to pay $3 for one cookie? **Give me a break!**
EXAMPLE 2: You expect me to believe that excuse? **Give me a break!**

NOTE: You might see this written in its informal, conversational form: "Gimme a break!" This is usually how the idiom is pronounced.

go ahead – to continue; to proceed without hesitation

EXAMPLE 1: We have more than enough food for dinner. **Go ahead** and invite your friend to join us.
EXAMPLE 2: Let's **go ahead** and buy our plane tickets now.

NOTE: "Go ahead" can also be used as a noun, as in the expression "to give somebody the go ahead," meaning to give somebody permission to move forward with an activity.

head over heels in love – very much in love

EXAMPLE 1: During the first years of their marriage, Brad and Jennifer were **head over heels in love** with each other.
EXAMPLE 2: Sara is **head over heels in love** with Mark. Unfortunately, he doesn't even know her name!

love at first sight – an immediate attraction

EXAMPLE 1: It took Allison several months to fall in love with Karl. It wasn't **love at first sight**.
EXAMPLE 2: Tony liked Tara immediately. It was **love at first sight**!

(to) make out – to kiss with much passion

EXAMPLE: Ted and Amber started **making out** at the stoplight and didn't realize that the light had turned green.

NOTE: "Make out" also means:
   1) To manage. How did you **make out** at the doctor's today?
   2) To understand or see with difficulty. It was so foggy, I could barely **make out** the street signs.
   3) To prepare a check or other payment. Please **make out** a check for this month's rent.

(to be) nuts about – to like very much

EXAMPLE 1 : Ted has every single Metallica album — he's **nuts about** that band.
EXAMPLE 2: We're just **nuts about** our new neighbors. We have them over for dinner once a month.

SYNONYM: crazy about

(to have a) one-track mind – having all thoughts directed to just one thing or activity; focused on just one thing

EXAMPLE 1: Ryan thinks about football all the time. He's got a **one-track mind**.
EXAMPLE 2: Mia has a **one-track-mind**. She thinks about boys all the time.

(to) plug away (at something) – to proceed with a boring or routine task; to keep trying

EXAMPLE 1: Only 842 more cookies to bake. Let's keep **plugging away**!
EXAMPLE 2: Don't give up on chemistry class. If you keep **plugging away**, you will eventually learn the material.

take a break – see *Lesson 13*

(to) treat (someone) like dirt – to behave in a nasty way towards someone; to treat someone poorly

EXAMPLE 1: Nobody was surprised when Nicole's boyfriend broke up with her, since she **treated him like dirt**.
EXAMPLE 2: I feel sorry for Jeffrey. The kids at school are very nasty to him. They really **treat him like dirt**.

✎ PRACTICE THE IDIOMS

Susan is telling the story of how she met her husband. Fill in the blanks, using the following idioms:

love at first sight	**go ahead**
plugging away	**treated him like dirt**
crunch time	**crank out**
making out	**crazy about**
broke up with	**head over heels in love**

I met Bob in college. He was in my English Literature class. I liked him right away. For me, it was _____. I wrote him several love poems, though I never gave them to him. Then I found out that he had a girlfriend. I saw him _____ _____with a girl named Joyce. It looked like she was _____ _____ Bob too. But later that week, I heard that she was a nasty person and that she _____. So I decided to _____ and ask him to the movies. He said he was too busy. It was _____, and he had to ____ _____ a paper for literature class and study for several exams. But I didn't give up. I kept _____. Then one day he _____ Joyce and asked me out to dinner. That was 25 years ago, and we're still together. Fortunately, we're still _____ with each other!

ANSWERS TO LESSON 14, p. 164

"Remember the rule of thumb –
imagine your audience naked."

NICOLE PRACTICES HER ELECTION SPEECH

Nicole is running for student body president. She must give a speech next week. She discusses the speech with her mother.

Susan: **What's up**, Nicole?

Nicole: I **pulled an all-nighter** working on my election speech.

Susan: **No wonder** you **look like** a **basket case**! Did you finish your speech?

Nicole: Yes, at 6 a.m.

Susan: That must be a **load off your mind**!

Nicole: It's not. I've got to give the speech tomorrow in front of 1,500 people. I'm a **nervous wreck**!

Susan: Just remember the old **rule of thumb**: Imagine your audience naked.

Nicole: That's gross. Why would I want to do that?

Susan: According to **conventional wisdom**, it'll make you less nervous.

Nicole: Only practice will **do the trick**.

Susan: Okay, let's hear the speech.

Nicole: Good afternoon, everyone. There are four candidates running for president. You think you have several choices. **In reality**, you have just one choice: me!

Susan: You can't say that. You'll **turn off** your audience immediately.

Nicole: It sounds like I have a **big head**?

Susan: **I'll say!**

IDIOMS – LESSON 15

basket case [slang] – someone or something in a useless or hopeless condition

EXAMPLE 1: After working a 12-hour day and then coming home and cooking dinner for her family, Tanya felt like a **basket case**.
EXAMPLE 2: After running the marathon, Brian felt like a **basket case**.

NOTE: You may also see the expression "economic basket case" to describe an economy that is doing very poorly. Example: After years of dictatorship, North Korea is an **economic basket case**.

(to have a) big head – arrogant; too proud of oneself

EXAMPLE 1: Stop bragging so much about the award you got at work! People will think you've got a **big head**.
EXAMPLE 2: Jenny has such a **big head**. No wonder nobody wants to be friends with her!

SYNONYM: to be full of oneself. Example: Joan is really **full of herself**. She's always talking about how smart she is.

conventional wisdom – a widely held belief

EXAMPLE 1: According to **conventional wisdom**, a diet high in salt can cause high blood pressure.
EXAMPLE 2: Challenging **conventional wisdom**, the psychologist said that sometimes it's healthy to be in a bad mood.

(to) do the trick – to achieve the desired results

EXAMPLE 1: Juan changed the light bulb and said, "That should **do the trick!**"

EXAMPLE 2: My house is difficult to find, so I'll put 10 large balloons on my mailbox on the day of the party. That should **do the trick**.

I'll say! – yes, definitely!

EXAMPLE 1: "Did you enjoy the Madonna concert?" – "**I'll say!**"

EXAMPLE 2: "Your sister must've been very happy after winning $50,000 in the lottery." – "**I'll say!**"

in reality – in fact; actually

EXAMPLE 1: Ted thinks it'll be easy to become a rock star. **In reality**, it will take years of hard work.

EXAMPLE 2: I know you think it'll be easy to get cheap tickets to a Broadway play. **In reality**, we'll have to wait in line for hours!

load off one's mind – a relief

EXAMPLE 1: When Amber called Ted to tell him that she arrived home safely, it was a big **load off his mind**.

EXAMPLE 2: Finishing her English essay was a **load off Nicole's mind**.

look like – have the appearance of

EXAMPLE 1: Before agreeing to go out on a date with her, Keith wanted to know what my cousin Maria **looked like**.

EXAMPLE 2: Please tell me what the cover of that new book **looks like** so it will be easier for me to find it in the bookstore.

NOTE: The expression "it looks like" can mean "it is likely that…"
Example: It's snowing, so **it looks like** the schools will be closed today.

nervous wreck – a person feeling very worried

EXAMPLE 1: Ted was a **nervous wreck** before his chemistry test.

EXAMPLE 2: Whenever Nicole rides on the back of her friend's motorcycle, Susan is a **nervous wreck**.

no wonder – it's not surprising

EXAMPLE 1: Brian's entire body is in pain. It's **no wonder** since he ran a marathon yesterday!

EXAMPLE 2: **No wonder** you're cold — it's January and you're walking around outside without a coat!

SYNONYM: small wonder

(to) pull an all-nighter – to stay up all night to do work

EXAMPLE 1: Ted **pulled an all-nighter** to study for his chemistry test and ended up falling asleep in class the next day.

EXAMPLE 2: I've got a 20-page paper due tomorrow morning, and I haven't even started writing it yet. I guess I'll be **pulling an all-nighter**!

rule of thumb – a useful principle

EXAMPLE 1: When cooking fish, a good **rule of thumb** is 10 minutes in the oven for each inch of thickness.

EXAMPLE 2: "Ted, as a **rule of thumb**, you should always plan to study for your chemistry tests for at least two hours."

(to) turn off – to cause to feel dislike or revulsion

EXAMPLE 1: I used to be friends with Monica, but she gossiped all the time and it really **turned me off**.

EXAMPLE 2: At first, Sara really liked Jacob. But when he started talking about all his ex-girlfriends, she was really **turned off**.

NOTE: The noun form, turn-off, is also common and usually describes something that causes the opposite sex to respond negatively. Example: When Jake started talking about all his ex-girlfriends, it was a real **turn-off** for Sara.

what's up? – *see Lesson 10*

✎ PRACTICE THE IDIOMS

Choose the best substitute for the phrase in bold:

1) Ted didn't start studying for his chemistry test until the night before. Then he had to **pull an all-nighter**.
   a) get plenty of rest before an exam
   b) stay up all night studying
   c) sleep late

2) After working on it for months, I finally gave my presentation this morning. That was certainly **a load off my mind**!
   a) a relief
   b) difficult
   c) easy

3) Nicole was **turned off** when Todd, her date, started picking his teeth with a toothpick during dinner.
   a) left the room
   b) became interested
   c) lost all interest

4) According to **conventional wisdom**, you shouldn't ask about salary on your first interview.
   a) accepted beliefs
   b) outdated beliefs
   c) smart people

5) Ted had to perform his music before one of the most important talent agents in the country. It's not surprising that he was **a nervous wreck**.
   a) confident
   b) very worried
   c) exhausted

6) Girls cheered and blew kisses whenever Ted performed his music. Amber worried that he'd **get a big head**.
   a) get a headache
   b) become arrogant
   c) find a new girlfriend

7) People keep telling Fred that he looks **like a basket case**. Maybe it's because he hasn't slept in weeks.
   a) really great
   b) angry
   c) terrible

8) Do you have a headache? Here, take two aspirin. That should **do the trick**.
   a) make you feel better
   b) perform magic
   c) make you feel worse

ANSWERS TO LESSON 15, p. 164

 *Review for Lessons 11-15*

Choose the best substitute for the phrase or sentence in bold:

1) Nicole didn't want to go to the party, but her friend **twisted her arm**.
   a) persuaded her
   b) hurt her arm
   c) agreed with her

2) Amber needs to go on a diet and lose 10 pounds, but it's difficult for her because **she has such a sweet tooth**.
   a) she has a loose tooth
   b) she has emotional problems
   c) she likes to eat sweets

3) Amber likes to design handbags as a hobby, but she's not sure she could **make a living at it**.
   a) do it for the rest of her life
   b) earn enough money to support herself
   c) do it all day long

4) Ted wanted to travel to Miami for a rock concert. His mother told him it was **out of the question**.
   a) a good idea
   b) still a possibility
   c) not a possibility

5) Nicole **worked her tail off**, making hundreds of posters for her campaign.
   a) worked very hard
   b) worked until her tail fell off
   c) made her friends work hard

6) **It's crunch time**. Ted has to write six papers in two days.
   a) It's a very busy time.
   b) It's a time to relax.
   c) It's a period of time filled with fun and laughter.

7) My 95-year old neighbor was cutting her grass on a hot summer day. I offered to **lend a hand**.
   a) give her my hand
   b) help her
   c) drive her to the hospital

8) Jennifer **treats her husband like dirt**. I don't know why he doesn't just leave her.
   a) is very nice to her husband
   b) asks her husband to do the gardening
   c) is nasty to her husband

9) Tattoos are **all the rage**. Many kids are getting them.
   a) something that makes you angry
   b) very popular
   c) easy to get

10) **Things are looking up for Bob**. He's already found a new job working for his wife.
   a) Bob's situation is getting worse.
   b) Bob's situation is improving.
   c) Bob always focuses on positive things.

11) Susan volunteered to host 45 exchange students from China. Now she fears she's **bitten off more than she can chew**.
   a) accepted an easy assignment
   b) taken on a bigger task than she can handle
   c) ordered too much Chinese food

12) If Ted doesn't **get going on** his chemistry homework soon, he's going to be up all night.
   a) start doing
   b) stop doing
   c) leave the house with

CROSSWORD PUZZLE

Across

2. My old job was boring. All I did was ____ numbers all day.
4. Bob went to the Village Market to get the ___ rolling on the cookie business.
5. You didn't take out the garbage yet? Never____! I'll do it myself.
7. Donna ate the whole apple pie herself. I guess she has a ____ tooth.
9. Jim never thought he could sell designer watches on street corners, but his brother taught him the ____ of the trade.
11. You've been working at the computer for hours. Why don't you take a ___?
12. After her boyfriend broke up with her, Anna was feeling down in the ___.
13. Mini-skirts were all the ____ last summer.

Down

1. Susan used to sing opera, but she hasn't sung in years. She's out of ____.
3. Bill thinks he's the smartest guy in the world. His friends think he just has a big ____.
6. I don't like horror movies, but John ____ my arm and I agreed to see *Murder on Main Street*.
8. My car wasn't running well so I changed the oil. That should do the ____.
10. After the car accident, Betty was a ____ wreck whenever she drove.
11. When I don't get eight hours of sleep, I feel like a ___ case in the morning.

ANSWERS TO REVIEW, p. 164

BOB BRINGS THE COOKIES TO THE VILLAGE MARKET

Bob brings Carol the cookies. He tells Carol that baking the cookies was easy because he had lots of help.

Carol: Bob, how did the baking go?

Bob: Slow **at first**, but we're **getting the hang of it**.

Carol: Once you **learn the ropes**, it becomes **second nature**.

Bob: **To tell you the truth,** I thought that baking 2,000 cookies would be a **pain in the neck**. But we managed to **round up** some helpers, and it was a **piece of cake**.

Carol: Well, thanks for coming **in person** with the cookies.

Bob: No problem. When will you need more?

Carol: It depends on how many we sell today.

Bob: How many do you think you'll sell?

Carol: Maybe 500, maybe 2,000. **Your guess is as good as mine. In any case,** I'll **keep you posted**.

Bob: Okay. Just **give me a ring** as soon as you know.

IDIOMS – LESSON 16

at first – in the beginning

EXAMPLE 1: Nicole didn't like *Don Quixote* **at first**, but after 200 pages she started to get into it.
EXAMPLE 2: Don't get discouraged if you don't succeed **at first**. The important thing is that you keep on trying!

(to) get the hang of (something) – to learn how to do something; to acquire an effective technique

EXAMPLE 1: Billy had trouble learning how to ride a bike, but after a few months he finally **got the hang of it**.
EXAMPLE 2: When I went snowboarding for the first time, I kept falling down. But after a while, I **got the hang of it**.

(to) give (someone) a ring – to telephone someone

EXAMPLE 1: **Give me a ring** tomorrow so we can discuss plans for this weekend.
EXAMPLE 2: If you're free on Saturday, **give me a ring** and we can go to the movies.

SYNONYM: to give (someone) a buzz [slang]

in any case – whatever the fact is; certainly

EXAMPLE 1: We can either go to the new Star Wars movie or see a play tonight. **In any case**, you'll need to be at my house by six o'clock.
EXAMPLE 2: You'll probably be too tired on Sunday to come over. **In any case**, give me a call in the morning to discuss.

in person – personally; in one's physical presence

EXAMPLE 1: Tim hoped that he and Svetlana would get along as well **in person** as they did over the Internet.
EXAMPLE 2: After hearing so much about Donna's boyfriend, I'm looking forward to meeting him **in person**.

(to) keep posted – to provide up-to-date information

EXAMPLE 1: **Keep me posted** about your plans for the summer. If you're going to be at your cottage on the lake, I'd love to come visit.
EXAMPLE 2: Good luck selling your house and **keep me posted**! I'd love to know how much you get for it.

(to) learn the ropes – to learn the basics

EXAMPLE 1: Mark **learned the ropes** of the restaurant business by working as a cook at Outback Steakhouse.

EXAMPLE 2: David worked at a big law firm for 10 years where he **learned the ropes**. Now he runs his own law firm.

pain in the neck – an annoyance

EXAMPLE 1: Yesterday I had to stay home all day and wait for the repairman. What a **pain in the neck**!

EXAMPLE 2: Alice wants me to drive her to the airport early tomorrow morning. That's going to be a **pain in the neck**!

piece of cake – very easy

EXAMPLE 1: Nicole finished her physics test in just 25 minutes. It was a **piece of cake**.

EXAMPLE 2: The driving test is a **piece of cake**. Don't worry about it.

SYNONYM: easy as pie. You should have no trouble passing the driving test. It's as **easy as pie**.

(to) round up – to gather people together

EXAMPLE 1: The town **rounded up** 200 volunteers to search for the hiker, who was lost in the woods of Yosemite National Park.

EXAMPLE 2: Let's **round up** some volunteers to help bake cookies and pies for the bake sale.

second nature – a behavior that has been practiced for so long, it seems to have been there always

EXAMPLE 1: Karen has been arguing with her husband every day for the past 20 years, so by now it's just **second nature**.

EXAMPLE 2: With practice, riding a unicycle becomes **second nature**.

to tell you the truth – to speak openly; to admit

EXAMPLE 1: **To tell you the truth,** Ted isn't a very good student.

EXAMPLE 2: **To tell you the truth,** I didn't even want to attend Katie's wedding. But I knew she'd be offended if I didn't go.

your guess is as good as mine – I don't know; I don't know any more than you do

EXAMPLE 1: Will we ever find intelligent life on other planets? **Your guess is as good as mine**.

EXAMPLE 2: Will Ted graduate on time? **Your guess is as good as mine**!

✎ Practice the Idioms

Fill in the blank with the appropriate word:

1) When Nicole drove her car for the first time, she was really nervous. Now, after an entire year, it's ____ nature.

    a) first   b) second   c) third

2) I can't believe I won. To ____ you the truth, I never thought I'd be able to beat you at tennis.

    a) say   b) tell   c) explain

3) Nicole was going to mail her college application to Yale. But then she decided to go to New Haven and deliver it ____ person.

    a) on   b) at   c) in

4) After a snowstorm, it can be a real pain in the ____ driving to work in the morning.

    a) head   b) arm   c) neck

5) The meeting in Dallas was canceled, but, in ____ case, we still need to go there.

    a) all   b) any   c) about

6) Starting a new job is difficult in the beginning. It gets easier once you learn the ____.

    a) ropes   b) chains   c) ties

7) Bob and Susan thought getting rich would be very difficult. But thanks to their cookie business, it was a piece of ____.

    a) cookie   b) cake   c) pie

8) Let's go to the movies tonight. I'll look in the newspaper and ____ you a ring after I see what's playing.

    a) offer   b) take   c) give

ANSWERS TO LESSON 16, p.165

CAROL TELLS BOB
THE GOOD NEWS

Carol phones Bob to tell him the cookies are selling very well and that she needs another 1,000 by the morning. Bob isn't sure he can make the cookies so quickly, but Carol insists.

Carol: Bob, your wife's cookies are **selling like hotcakes**!

Bob: How many did you sell, Carol?

Carol: We've **sold out**. I need more **right away**! Bring me another 1,000 by tomorrow at 9 a.m.

Bob: That's a **tall order**, Carol.

Carol: Don't **blow it**, Bob! Susan's Scrumptious Cookies could really **take off**.

Bob: I know, but I'm not sure we have enough time to bake all those cookies.

Carol: Bake all night if you have to. **Burn the midnight oil**! If you work hard now, you'll be **sitting pretty** in a few years.

Bob: **Rest assured** that I'll **do my best** to **deliver the goods**.

Carol: Okay, now let's stop the **chitchat**. You've got work to do!

IDIOMS – LESSON 17

(to) blow it – to spoil an opportunity

EXAMPLE 1: The actress got nervous and forgot all of her lines. She really **blew it!**
EXAMPLE 2: I'll give you one more chance, but don't **blow it** this time!

SYNONYM: to screw up [slang]. Example: I can't believe you **screwed up** during the interview by asking for six weeks of vacation before you even got the job offer!

(to) burn the midnight oil – to stay up late studying or working

EXAMPLE 1: Michael **burned the midnight oil** studying for his algebra test.
EXAMPLE 2: The project is due tomorrow and we're far from finished. We're going to have to **burn the midnight oil** tonight.

chitchat – casual conversation; gossip

EXAMPLE 1: Peter told Heather to stop the **chitchat** and get back to work.
EXAMPLE 2: Okay, enough **chitchat!** Let's start discussing this week's reading assignment.

SYNONYM: to shoot the breeze

NOTE: Chitchat can also be a verb. Example: Amber and Ted were **chit-chatting** all night long.

(to) deliver the goods – to meet expectations; to do what's required

EXAMPLE 1: Peter thought Bob wasn't **delivering the goods,** so he fired him.
EXAMPLE 2: I'm depending on you to finish the job on time. I know that you can **deliver the goods!**

SYNONYM: to cut the mustard. Example: If you can't **cut the mustard** here, you'll have to find a new job.

(to) do one's best – to try as hard as possible

EXAMPLE 1: Although Ted **did his best**, he still failed his chemistry test.
EXAMPLE 2: You might not get a perfect score on your history test, but just **do your best**.

SYNONYM: to give it one's all

rest assured – be sure

EXAMPLE 1: **Rest assured** that the police will find the thieves.
EXAMPLE 2: **Rest assured** I'll take good care of your dog while you're on vacation.

right away – immediately

EXAMPLE 1: When Meg realized her house was on fire, she called the fire department **right away**.
EXAMPLE 2: You need some sugar for your cookies? I'll bring some over **right away**.

(to) sell like hotcakes – to sell fast; to be a popular item

EXAMPLE 1: Those new Fubu blue jeans are **selling like hotcakes**. All the girls love them.
EXAMPLE 2: Stephen King's new novel is **selling like hotcakes**.

(to be) sitting pretty – in a good position (often financially)

EXAMPLE 1: After Chad won the lottery, he was really **sitting pretty**. He quit his job and bought a mansion in Malibu, California.
EXAMPLE 2: Gina was one of the first people to work at Amazon.com, and she made millions on her stock options. Now she's **sitting pretty**.

sold out – completely sold

EXAMPLE 1: Becky was really disappointed when she found out that the Britney Spears concert was **sold out**.
EXAMPLE 2: Susan's cookies were very popular at the bake sale. In fact, they **sold out** in just 20 minutes!

(to) take off – to become popular; to grow suddenly

EXAMPLE: Julia Roberts' career **took off** with the film "Pretty Woman."

NOTE: "Take off" has several other meanings:
1. Remove. Please **take off** your shoes before coming inside our apartment. We just vacuumed this morning.
2. To leave. We're **taking off** now. See you later!
3. To deduct. The waiter forgot to bring us drinks, so he **took $10 off** the bill.
4. To leave the ground. The airplane **took off** on time.

tall order – a task or goal that is difficult to achieve

EXAMPLE 1: It'll be a **tall order** to find a new governor as popular as the current one.
EXAMPLE 2: You want me to figure out how to clone your pet rabbit? That's a **tall order**!

Choose the most appropriate reply to the following statements:

1) "Bob, your cookies are delicious. They're selling like hotcakes."

   Bob's reply:
   a) "I'm not surprised. My family has always loved them."
   b) "What? I thought people would buy more."
   c) "Yes, they are best when served hot."

2) "Bob, I know you can get me 1,000 cookies by morning. Don't blow it!"

   Bob's reply:
   a) "I never blow on the cookies. I let them cool down by themselves."
   b) "Don't worry. I'll be sure to get you the cookies by 9 a.m."
   c) "Thanks. I'll take my time then."

3) "Bob, I've got some great news for you. All of your chocolate chip cookies have sold out!"

   Bob's reply:
   a) "Great. I'd better make more."
   b) "I guess people don't like them."
   c) "How many are left?"

4) "Ted, if you and Amber don't stop the chitchat, you'll never finish your homework."

   Ted's reply:
   a) "Okay, we'll stay up all night talking."
   b) "Okay, we'll stop talking and start hitting the books."
   c) "Yes, Amber is helping a lot with my homework."

5) "Ted, ask Amber to come over right away to help bake cookies."

   Ted's reply:
   a) "Okay. I'll tell her to come over next Saturday."
   b) "Okay. I'll tell her to come over immediately."
   c) "Okay. I'll ask her to go away."

6) "Bob, if you work hard now, you'll be sitting pretty in a couple of years."

   Bob's reply:
   a) "Thank you. I am looking forward to feeling pretty."
   b) "I don't enjoy sitting for long periods of time."
   c) "Great. I'd love to be able to stop working and start relaxing more."

7) "Nicole, getting elected to the United States Senate is a very tall order."

   Nicole's reply:
   a) "I know, but I love a good challenge."
   b) "I agree. It should be very easy."
   c) "I know. I've already put in my order."

8) "Bob, I suggest you burn the midnight oil and make 1,000 cookies tonight."

   Bob's reply:
   a) "Okay. I'll go to sleep at midnight and wake up at 10 a.m."
   b) "Yes, we'll need quite a bit of oil for the cookies."
   c) "Okay. I'll work all night and finish up by morning."

ANSWERS TO LESSON 17, p. 165

EVERYONE BAKES COOKIES

Bob tells his family the cookies are selling well. He asks his kids to help bake more cookies for tomorrow. Nicole says she's too busy to lend a hand.

Bob: The cookies are **selling like hotcakes**!

Ted: **Way to go**, Dad!

Bob: I need you kids to **help out** tonight with the cookies. We need another thousand by morning.

Nicole: One thousand by tomorrow morning? That's impossible!

Ted: Amber and I will **lend a hand**. She's a real **night owl**, so she won't mind **staying up** late.

Bob: Nicole, we'll need your help too.

Nicole: Bake cookies the night before the elections? **Nothing doing**!

Ted: **Lighten up**, **big shot**! You're running for high school president, not President of the United States.

Nicole: Ted, you really **get on my nerves** sometimes.

Bob: Okay, kids, let's stop **fooling around**. We need to **get the show on the road**!

IDIOMS – LESSON 18

big shot – a powerful or important person

EXAMPLE 1: Martin has become a real **big shot** in Hollywood. This year he produced several movies.
EXAMPLE 2: Adam is a **big shot** in Silicon Valley. He started a very successful software company.

NOTE: This expression can also be used in the negative sense, to mean somebody who *thinks* they're very important. Example: Now that she's been promoted to vice president, Beth thinks she's such a **big shot**!

(to) fool around – to waste time, or spend it in a silly way

EXAMPLE 1: If we keep **fooling around** here, we'll be late to the restaurant!
EXAMPLE 2: Stop **fooling around**! You've got lots of work to do.

NOTE: This expression also can mean to have casual sexual relations. Example: Steve and Tanya were **fooling around** in the back seat of the car when a policeman knocked on the window.

(to) get on one's nerves – to annoy or irritate someone

EXAMPLE 1: My neighbor's dog barks all night. It really **gets on my nerves**.
EXAMPLE 2: Please stop whistling. It's **getting on my nerves**!

SYNONYMS: to get under someone's skin; to bug someone [slang]

(to) get the show on the road – to start working; to begin an undertaking

EXAMPLE 1: We can't afford to waste any more time — let's **get the show on the road**!
EXAMPLE 2: Kids, let's **get the show on the road**. We don't want to be late for the movie!

(to) help out – *see Lesson 12*

(to) lend a hand – *see Lesson 13*

(to) lighten up – to stop taking things so seriously

EXAMPLE 1: **Lighten up!** I'm sure Ted was only joking when he said your guitar playing gave him a headache.
EXAMPLE 2: Don always takes his job so seriously. He needs to **lighten up**.

SYNONYMS: chill out [slang]; take it easy

night owl – a person who enjoys being active late at night

EXAMPLE 1: Sara goes to sleep every night at 3 a.m. She's a real **night owl**.
EXAMPLE 2: I never go to bed before midnight. I'm a **night owl**.

Nothing doing! – Not a chance!

EXAMPLE 1: You want me to buy the Golden Gate Bridge from you for a million bucks? **Nothing doing**!
EXAMPLE 2: You want me to write your paper on Catherine the Great? **Nothing doing!**

SYNONYMS: No way! Not on your life!

(to) sell like hotcakes – *see Lesson 17*

(to) stay up – not to go to bed; to stay awake

EXAMPLE 1: Ted and Amber **stayed up** all night talking about cookies.
EXAMPLE 2: Whenever I **stay up** late, I regret it the next morning.

Way to go! – *see Lesson 4*

✎ PRACTICE THE IDIOMS

Fill in the blank with the appropriate word:

1) I was really proud of my friend for winning an Olympic medal. "Way to _____!" I told her.

   a) do   b) succeed   c) go

2) Amber loves to cook, so she never minds lending _____ in the kitchen.

   a) herself   b) a hand   c) her hands

3) Vanessa is definitely not a night _____. She likes to be in bed by nine o'clock every night.

   a) bird   b) hawk   c) owl

4) After Mr. Digby was elected president of the company, he thought he was a real _____ shot.

   a) big   b) huge   c) large

5) You're taking everything too seriously. You need to lighten
___.

   a) above   b) up   c) down

6) Let's go! We're already late. Let's get the show on the _____.

   a) street   b) way   c) road

7) When people near me whisper during a movie, it really ___
on my nerves.

   a) gets   b) acts   c) scratches

8) Nicole's teacher asked her to help a new exchange student
from Argentina with her English homework. Nicole was
happy to help _____.

   a) around   b) out   c) in

✪ BONUS PRACTICE

Choose the best substitute for the phrase or sentence in bold:

1) You want me to drive you all the way to Toronto during this
snowstorm? **Nothing doing!**
   a) Great idea!
   b) No problem!
   c) Not a chance!

2) Len and Ben, college roommates, **stayed up** until 3 a.m. talking and drinking beer. No wonder they didn't wake up until
noon the next day!
   a) didn't go to bed
   b) went to bed
   c) didn't eat dinner

3) Michael used to work the late shift at McDonald's — from midnight to 8 a.m. He didn't mind since he's **a night owl**.
   a) a wise person
   b) a person who goes to sleep early
   c) a person who likes to stay up late

4) The man behind me on the bus wouldn't stop whistling. It really **got on my nerves**!
   a) entertained me
   b) annoyed me
   c) relaxed me

5) Our plane leaves in just two hours. If we don't **get the show on the road**, we're going to miss it.
   a) go into the street
   b) get ready to go
   c) call the airline

6) You want to attend Yale University? Call my friend Penny. She's **a real big shot** on the admissions committee.
   a) a powerful person
   b) a big mouth
   c) a useless person

7) Ted was **fooling around** with his friends when he should've been studying for his chemistry test.
   a) acting like a fool
   b) putting time to good use
   c) wasting time

8) You got a big promotion at work? **Way to go!**
   a) Too bad!
   b) Good job!
   c) Sorry to hear that!

ANSWERS TO LESSON 18, p. 165

NICOLE'S CLOSE ELECTION

Nicole loses the election at school. She doesn't want to accept it, so she looks for excuses. Ted encourages her to accept defeat and move on.

Nicole: I lost the election **by a hair** — just 10 votes! But I'm not **giving up**.

Ted: **Give me a break**, Nicole. You lost. **Live with it**!

Nicole: But I was a **sure thing**! If I hadn't stayed up so late baking cookies, I wouldn't have **messed up** my speech.

Ted: **Get real**, Nicole.

Nicole: It's your fault, Ted. I lost because your friends didn't vote for me!

Ted: Don't try to **put the blame on** me! I **gave it my best shot**.

Nicole: They must've made a mistake while counting the votes. I'll demand a re-count on Monday and **set the record straight**.

Ted: Don't **make a fool of yourself**, Nicole. **Face it,** Andrea won the election **fair and square**!

Nicole: Well, I just don't know where I **went wrong**.

Susan: Here, take a chocolate chip cookie. That'll **cheer you up for sure**!

IDIOMS – LESSON 19

by a hair – just barely; very narrowly; by a small amount

EXAMPLE 1: Larry won the bicycle race **by a hair**. The second-place winner came in just a second behind him.
EXAMPLE 2: Was the tennis ball in or out? I think it was out **by a hair**. You know the old saying: "When in doubt, call it out!"

(to) cheer up – *see Lesson 6*

Face it – *see Lesson 1*

fair and square – honestly

EXAMPLE 1: Did George Bush win the 2000 presidential election **fair and square**? That depends on whether you ask a Democrat or a Republican!
EXAMPLE 2: Tony won the ping pong tournament **fair and square**.

for sure – definitely

EXAMPLE 1: This year, Tom Cruise will win an Academy Award **for sure**.
EXAMPLE 2: Mike is the most popular guy in school. If he runs for student body president, he'll win **for sure**.

Get real – *see Lesson 3*

(to) give it one's best shot – to try as hard as one can

EXAMPLE 1: Courtney lost the race, but at least she **gave it her best shot**.
EXAMPLE 2: I know you're nervous about the interview. Just **give it your best shot** and see what happens.

give me a break – *see Lesson 14*

(to) give up – to admit defeat; to surrender

EXAMPLE 1: Bill **gave up** golf after realizing he'd never be good at it.
EXAMPLE 2: I know you're 100 points ahead of me, but I still might win the Scrabble game. I'm not **giving up** yet!

(to) go wrong – to make a mistake; to go astray; to malfunction; to work incorrectly

EXAMPLE 1: Follow the directions I gave you, and you can't **go wrong**.
EXAMPLE 2: Something **went wrong** with my neighbor's car alarm system, and the alarm wouldn't stop ringing all night.

(to) live with it – to accept a difficult reality

EXAMPLE 1: Your boss is an idiot. **Live with it.**
EXAMPLE 2: Your hair will never be straight. Just **live with it!**

NOTE: There is also the expression "to learn to live with it," which means to get used to something annoying or difficult. Example: Sandra knew that Roger would always throw his dirty clothes on the floor. She'd just have to **learn to live with it**.

(to) make a fool of oneself – to cause oneself to look stupid

EXAMPLE 1: Dan drank too much and then **made a fool of himself**.
EXAMPLE 2: Please stop arguing with me in front of all these people. You're **making a fool of yourself!**

(to) mess up – to make a mistake; to spoil an opportunity

EXAMPLE 1: Amber **messed up** and put salt instead of sugar in the cookies.
EXAMPLE 2: Ted really **messed up** on his chemistry test. He got a "D."

SYNONYM: screw up [slang]

(to) put the blame on (someone) – to name somebody else as responsible for a misdeed or misfortune

EXAMPLE 1: Mrs. Lopez **put the blame on** her husband for losing their life savings in the stock market.
EXAMPLE 2: Don't **put the blame on me** that your plants died while you were on vacation. You forgot to tell me to water them!

(to) set the record straight – to correct an inaccurate account

EXAMPLE 1: Ken knew his father was innocent, and he hoped he could **set the record straight** one day.
EXAMPLE 2: Let me **set the record straight**. I won the last game.

sure thing – an outcome that is assured

EXAMPLE 1: Gary bet all his money on a horse named Trixie, thinking she was a **sure thing**.
EXAMPLE 2: Nicole has a good chance of getting accepted to Yale, but it's still not a **sure thing**.

✒ PRACTICE THE IDIOMS

Ted is angry at Nicole because she didn't do a good job on his chemistry homework. Fill in the blanks using the following idioms:

give me a break	**cheer you up**
sure thing	**for sure**
put the blame on me	**live with it**
give it my best shot	**messed up**

Ted: Nicole, my teacher gave me back my chemistry homework. I got a terrible grade! I thought _____ you'd help me get an "A+."

Nicole: I'm sorry. I really did _____, but I guess it wasn't good enough.

Ted: Not good enough? That's right. You really _____ _____!

Nicole: You never should've asked me to do your homework. Don't try to _____ for your bad grades.

Ted: Yes, my mistake. I thought you were a _____ _____!

Nicole: So you'll get a bad grade in chemistry. Just learn to _____. Here, take one of Mom's cookies. It'll help _____.

Ted: You think a stupid cookie will cheer me up? _____ _____!

ANSWERS TO LESSON 19, p. 165

120

BOB GETS AN ANGRY CALL FROM CAROL

Carol calls Bob to tell him that a customer found a hair in her cookie. Bob wants Carol to forget about this, but Carol thinks it's very serious. She refuses to buy any more cookies from Bob.

Carol: Bob, a lady came into the Village Market today **ranting and raving**.

Bob: Oh yeah? What happened?

Carol: She found a blue hair in her chocolate chip cookie!

Bob: Aha. I can see how she'd be **taken aback.**

Carol: Does anybody in your family have blue hair?

Bob: **As a matter of fact**, my son's girlfriend Amber has blue hair.

Carol: Bob, I can't sell your cookies anymore.

Bob: Aren't you **blowing things out of proportion**?

Carol: The health department would **throw the book at me** if they **found out** about this.

Bob: Couldn't we just **sweep this under the rug?**

Carol: No. This is too serious.

Bob: But I was just **getting a handle on** the cookie business. Now what will I do? I don't have any other way of **making a living!**

Carol: **My heart goes out to you,** Bob, but you need to **get your act together.** I want to sell *chocolate chip* cookies, not *hair* cookies!

Bob: I guess I just **knocked myself out** for the past week for nothing.

Carol: Clearly!

IDIOMS – LESSON 20

as a matter of fact – in fact; actually

EXAMPLE 1: We need more milk? **As a matter of fact**, I was just going to ask you to go shopping.
EXAMPLE 2: This isn't the first time Andy has gotten in trouble at school. **As a matter of fact**, just last month he was suspended for an entire week.

(to) blow things out of proportion – to exaggerate; to make more of something than one should

EXAMPLE 1: They sent a 12 year-old boy to jail for biting his babysitter? Don't you think they're **blowing things out of proportion**?
EXAMPLE 2: Sally called the police when her neighbor's party got too loud. I think that was **blowing things out of proportion**.

SYNONYM: To make a mountain out of a molehill

(to) find out – to learn; to discover

EXAMPLE 1: Al is calling the theater to **find out** what time the movie starts.
EXAMPLE 2: David had a big party at his house while his parents were away on vacation. Fortunately for him, they never **found out**.

(to) get a handle on – to gain an understanding of

EXAMPLE 1: This new computer program is very difficult. I still haven't **gotten a handle on** it.

EXAMPLE 2: Once you **get a handle on** how the game works, please explain it to everybody else.

(to) get one's act together – to get organized; to start operating more effectively

EXAMPLE 1: If Ted **gets his act together** now, he might be able to get into a good college.

EXAMPLE 2: We'd better **get our act together**. Otherwise, we're going to miss our flight.

(to) knock oneself out – to work very hard at something (sometimes too hard)

EXAMPLE 1: Ted **knocked himself out** getting votes for Nicole, and she didn't even say thank you.

EXAMPLE 2: I really **knocked myself out** getting these free concert tickets for you and your girlfriend. I hope you appreciate it.

NOTE: "Don't knock yourself out!" means don't work too hard at something or for someone; it's not worth it. Example: **Don't knock yourself out** for Jeremy — he won't appreciate it anyway!

(to) make a living – *see Lesson 11*

one's heart goes out to (someone) – to feel sorry for someone

EXAMPLE 1: **My heart goes out to the Richardsons**. Their home was destroyed in a fire.

EXAMPLE 2: Naomi's **heart went out to all the people** who lost their jobs when the auto plant shut down.

(to) rant and rave – to talk loudly, often in anger

EXAMPLE 1: A customer in the video rental store was **ranting and raving** that the DVD he rented was broken.

EXAMPLE 2: Please stop **ranting and raving**! Let's discuss this issue in a calm manner.

(to) sweep (something) under the rug – to hide something, often a scandal

EXAMPLE 1: "Senator, don't try to **sweep it under the rug**. Everybody knows about your affair with the intern."

EXAMPLE 2: Let's just **sweep this incident under the rug** and move on.

taken aback – surprised (almost always in a negative sense)

EXAMPLE 1: Nicole was **taken aback** when her friend Rosa told her she no longer wanted to hang out with her.

EXAMPLE 2: I was **taken aback** when my friend asked me if she could borrow my toothbrush because she forgot hers at home.

(to) throw the book at someone – to punish or chide severely

EXAMPLE 1: When Ted failed his chemistry test the second time, his teacher really **threw the book at him**.

EXAMPLE 2: The judge **threw the book at Matt** for stealing a football from the store. He'll be going to jail for six months.

✍ PRACTICE THE IDIOMS

Choose the best substitute for the phrase in bold:

1) After Nicole lost the election, she started **ranting and raving.**
   a) complaining loudly
   b) speaking quietly
   c) asking many questions

2) When a stranger approached me on the bus and asked to borrow my cell phone, I was **taken aback**.
   a) disappointed
   b) surprised
   c) delighted

3) When George showed up for work five minutes late, his boss Beth threatened to fire him. Beth is known for **blowing things out of proportion**.
   a) making a big deal out of small things
   b) lying
   c) creating extra work for someone

4) My apartment is always messy. I need to **get my act together** and start cleaning it once a week.
   a) start pretending
   b) gather a group of people together
   c) get organized

5) **My heart goes out to** all the homeless people lying outside my apartment building in February.
   a) I help
   b) I feel sorry for
   c) I feel good about

6) I just **found out** yesterday that Amber never washes her hands before making cookies. Ted told me.
   a) saw
   b) overheard
   c) learned

7) The judge is going to **throw the book at Jim** for robbing several houses.
   a) release Jim from jail
   b) charge Jim with an offense
   c) read to Jim

8) Ted's chemistry homework was much more difficult than Nicole had expected. She just couldn't seem to **get a handle on it**.
   a) finish it
   b) understand it
   c) hold it in her hands

   ANSWERS TO LESSON 20, p. 165

 Review for Lessons 16-20

Fill in the blank with the appropriate word:

1) My aunt and uncle are really sitting _____. They made a lot of money in the stock market.

   a) rich   b) poor   c) pretty

2) Lighten ____! You need to stop taking your job so seriously.

    a) it   b) up   c) over

3) After a week, my houseguests really started to get ____ my nerves. They made long-distance phone calls to Singapore, drank all my wine, and slept until noon every day.

    a) by   b) in   c) on

4) Amber likes to stay up past midnight every night. She's what you'd call a ____ owl.

    a) night   b) busy   c) day

5) Mildred thought she'd have trouble remembering to take her pills. But now, after ten months, it's ____ nature.

    a) first   b) second   c) third

6) Susan messed ____ and left the cookies in the oven for 25 minutes too long. They were ruined.

    a) up   b) over   c) away

7) Andrea didn't cheat. She won the election fair and ____.

    a) easily   b) circle   c) square

8) Bob didn't know anything about baking when he and Susan started selling cookies, but he quickly learned the ____.

    a) chains   b) ropes   c) strings

9) Ted and his friends were fooling ____ in the chemistry laboratory when they accidentally started a fire.

    a) around   b) about   c) away

10) Mary's daughter wanted the new Harry Potter book. But by the time they got to the bookstore, it was already sold ____.

    a) out   b) in   c) away

CROSSWORD PUZZLE

Across
2. Senator Brown's re-election would have been a sure ____ if he hadn't gotten caught stealing candy at Wal-Mart.
3. Chad is sitting ____. He just won the lottery.
6. Nicole had to burn the ____ oil to finish her English paper by the morning.
8. When Ted was caught copying his friend's math homework, his teacher wasn't willing to sweep it under the ____.
10. It takes time to learn the ____ when you start a new job.
11. Once you do it a few times, riding a unicycle is a piece of ____.
12. My friend's dog kept licking my hand. It was getting on my ____.

Down
1. Carly is a real big ____. She runs a large corporation.
4. Some people in restaurants like to ____ and rave when their soup is too cold.
5. I tried to give my friend a ____ this morning, but she wasn't home. I got her answering machine.
7. My ____ goes out to people who live in America, but don't speak any English.
8. Martha Stewart tried to set the ____ straight during her television interview with Barbara Walters.
9. Filling out tax forms is a pain in the ____.

ANSWERS TO REVIEW, p. 166

SUSAN GETS A SURPRISE CALL

Donna from the National Cookie Company calls Susan. She wants to buy out Susan's Scrumptious Cookies. Susan is very happy.

Susan: Hello?

Donna: Good afternoon. Are you Susan, of Susan's Scrumptious Cookies?

Susan: Yes, I am.

Donna: My name is Donna Jenkins, and I'm calling from the National Cookie Company. We're **nuts about** your cookies, and we'd like to sell them **all over** the country.

Susan: Unfortunately, we're running **on a shoestring** out of our kitchen. We can't make enough cookies for you.

Donna: My company wants to buy the recipe and the brand name from you.

Susan: Oh yeah? Why would you want to do that?

Donna: We have a successful **track record** of buying small companies and turning them into big ones.

Susan: **In that case**, I'm sure we can **come to an agreement**.

Donna: Great. You just **made my day**!

Susan: You'll need to **work out** the **nuts and bolts** of the agreement with my husband. He's the business manager.

Donna: May I speak with him now?

Susan: He's at a meeting. I'll have him get **in touch with** you when he returns.

Donna: Good. I **look forward to** speaking with him.

IDIOMS – LESSON 21

all over – throughout; everywhere

EXAMPLE 1: Nicole's classmates are from **all over** the world, including Argentina, Brazil, China, Japan, Korea, Poland, and Ukraine.
EXAMPLE 2: Oh no! I got ketchup **all over** my white sweater.

(to) come to an agreement – to reach an agreement

EXAMPLE 1: If we can **come to an agreement** now, I can start work on Monday.
EXAMPLE 2: If you're not willing to negotiate, it's going to be very difficult for us to **come to an agreement**.

in that case – under that circumstance

EXAMPLE 1: It's snowing? **In that case**, you'd better take the bus to school today instead of driving.
EXAMPLE 2: You forgot your wallet at home today? **In that case**, you can borrow five bucks from me for lunch.

(to be *or* to get) in touch with (someone) – to be *or* to get in contact with (someone)

EXAMPLE 1: I was surprised when Luis called me, since we hadn't been **in touch with each other** since high school.
EXAMPLE 2: Leave me your contact information in case I need to **get in touch with you** while you're on vacation.

(to) look forward to – to anticipate eagerly

EXAMPLE 1: I'm **looking forward to** my trip to Mexico next month.
EXAMPLE 2: Ron has worked as a high school teacher for over 40 years. He's really **looking forward to** retiring next year.

(to) make one's day – to give one great satisfaction

EXAMPLE 1: Our neighbors with the crazy dogs are moving away? That really **makes my day**!
EXAMPLE 2: Thanks for bringing over those cookies last week. That **made my day**!

(to be) nuts about – *see Lesson 14*

nuts and bolts – details; basic components of something

EXAMPLE 1: I don't need to know the **nuts and bolts** of how the computer works — just show me how to turn it on.
EXAMPLE 2: Simon really understands the **nuts and bolts** of how toilets work. He would be a very good plumber.

on a shoestring – on a very low budget

EXAMPLE 1: Bob and Susan were living **on a shoestring** after Bob lost his job.
EXAMPLE 2: In the beginning, the Hewlett-Packard company ran **on a shoestring** out of a garage.

track record – a record of achievements or performances

EXAMPLE 1: The women's basketball team at the University of Connecticut has an excellent **track record**.
EXAMPLE 2: We've spoken to your past employers, so we know you've got an excellent **track record**.

(to) work out – to find a solution; to resolve

EXAMPLE 1: Nicole spent half the night helping Ted **work out** a very difficult chemistry problem.
EXAMPLE 2: Sally couldn't **work out** her problems with her neighbors, so she finally decided to move away.

NOTE: "Work out" has several other meanings, including:
1. succeed; prove effective. This plan won't **work out** — you'll need to go back to the drawing board and work out a new plan.
2. endure; last. Tony and Angela argue all the time. I don't think their marriage will **work out**.
3. exercise. After **working out** at the gym for two hours, Scott could barely walk.

✎ PRACTICE THE IDIOMS

Fill in the blank with the appropriate word:

1) There's a handsome exchange student from Sweden at Nicole's school this year. Nicole is nuts ____ him.

    a) with   b) into   c) about

2) Susan and Bob were able to come ____ an agreement with the representative from the National Cookie Company.

    a) from   b) with   c) to

3) When somebody has a successful track ____ , it's usually easy for them to find a new job.

    a) record   b) history   c) past

4) Let's have dinner on Saturday night. I'll get in touch ____ you later to choose a restaurant.

    a) from   b) by   c) with

5) Susan doesn't have a lot of money. In fact, she's running her business ____ a shoestring.

    a) with   b) on   c) in

6) You can find Starbucks coffee houses all ____ the country, from New York to California.

    a) over   b) above   c) within

7) Bob hasn't been on vacation in years. He's really looking ____ to his trip to Maine.

    a) above   b) forward   c) ahead

8) Ted's teacher helped him work ____ a study schedule.

    a) out   b) in   c) through

ANSWERS TO LESSON 21, p. 166

SUSAN SHARES THE GOOD NEWS

Bob tells Susan that the Village Market won't take their cookies anymore. Susan tells Bob that the National Cookie Company wants to buy out Susan's Scrumptious Cookies.

Bob: Dear, I've got some bad news.

Susan: **What's the matter**, Bob?

Bob: The Village Market won't take any more of our cookies.

Susan: Why not? They're **selling like hotcakes**!

Bob: I know, but a lady found a blue hair in her cookie. Now Carol refuses to sell them.

Susan: Carol is such a **dragon lady**! We're **better off** having **nothing to do with her**.

Bob: She's not my **cup of tea** either, but she was selling lots of cookies.

Susan: Oh well. **That's the way the cookie crumbles**. Ha ha. **Get it?**

Bob: Susan, this is **no laughing matter**!

Susan: Bob, we don't need the Village Market anymore.

Bob: Why not?

Susan: The National Cookie Company called. They want to **buy out** our business.

Bob: Susan, this is a **dream come true. It looks like** we've **struck it rich**!

Susan: Yes. Soon we'll be **rolling in dough**!

IDIOMS – LESSON 22

better off – in a more fortunate position

EXAMPLE 1: We're **better off** leaving for France on Thursday evening, so we can spend the entire weekend there.
EXAMPLE 2: If you're interested in studying languages, you'd be **better off** attending Northwestern University than the University of Chicago.

NOTE: This expression is often used with conditional tense (would), especially when you're giving advice: "you *would be* better off doing something" or "*you'd be* better off doing something."

(to) buy out – to purchase an entire business or someone's share of a business

EXAMPLE 1: Microsoft **bought out** Adam's company for $12 million.
EXAMPLE 2: Harriett and Jane sell homemade snack chips. They hope one day a big company will **buy out** their business.

cup of tea – *see Lesson 5*

dragon lady – a nasty woman who misuses her power

EXAMPLE 1: Beth is a real **dragon lady**. She's always screaming at her employees and blaming them for her mistakes. I hope she gets fired!
EXAMPLE 2: Liz was nasty to you? I'm not surprised. She's a **dragon lady**.

SYNONYMS: bitch [slang]; shrew

(to) get it – to understand

EXAMPLE 1: I invited 40 people to my Thanksgiving dinner, but only 10 people came. I don't **get it**!
EXAMPLE 2: Don't you **get it**? Your company is about to go out of business!

it looks like – it's likely that

EXAMPLE 1: **It looks like** I'll be able to get out of work early today, so let's plan on meeting downtown at 4:30.
EXAMPLE 2: **It looks like** it's going to rain, so we'd better just cancel the picnic now.

no laughing matter – nothing to joke about; something serious

EXAMPLE 1: When the tornado came into town, it was **no laughing matter**.
EXAMPLE 2: Jim might have been fooling around when he hit John, but he really hurt him. It was **no laughing matter**.

nothing to do with (someone *or* something) – not have any relationship with someone; to not get involved with something

EXAMPLE 1: After I found out that Nora shoplifted some lipstick from the drugstore, I wanted **nothing to do with her**.
EXAMPLE 2: Larry asked Nick if he wanted to help him plan a robbery. Nick told Larry that he wanted **nothing to do with it**.

rolling in dough – very rich

EXAMPLE 1: Susan and Bob don't need to work anymore. They're **rolling in dough**.
EXAMPLE 2: Adam will be able to retire young. He's **rolling in dough**.

NOTE: This is a play on words. "Dough" means "money" as well as what is used to make cookies, breads, and pastries. The dough (cookies) made by Bob and Susan brought them lots of dough (money).

SYNONYMS: rolling in it; rolling in money; loaded

(to) sell like hotcakes – *see Lesson 17*

(to) strike it rich – to attain sudden financial success

EXAMPLE 1: Chad **struck it rich** with the winning lottery ticket.
EXAMPLE 2: Craig hopes to **strike it rich** so he can quit his job and open a winery in California.

that's the way the cookie crumbles – that's the way things go sometimes and there's nothing you can do about it

EXAMPLE 1: You lost your job? **That's the way the cookie crumbles**.
EXAMPLE 2: Somebody drank your last can of Pepsi? Oh well, **that's the way the cookie crumbles**.

What's the matter? – *see Lesson 2*

Choose the best substitute for the phrase or sentence in bold:

1) "**What's the matter**? You don't look happy."
   a) How are you?
   b) What does it mean?
   c) What's wrong?

2) We sold our business. Now **we're rolling in dough**!
   a) we're still making cookies
   b) we're rich
   c) we're poor

3) How could a woman find a hair in her cookie? **I just don't get it**.
   a) I don't understand it.
   b) I don't get hair in my cookies.
   c) I don't believe it.

4) Ted and Amber think they're going to **strike it rich** in the music business.
   a) get hurt
   b) make lots of money
   c) hit something

5) Bob thought that losing his job at the furniture store was **no laughing matter**.
   a) something serious
   b) something to laugh about
   c) something that doesn't really matter

6) My boss at the plastics company was a real **dragon lady**. Whenever I went into her office, she started yelling.
   a) ugly woman
   b) nasty woman
   c) fire-breathing monster

7) Nicole, I'm sorry you lost the election for president, but **that's the way the cookie crumbles**.
   a) that's how it goes and you can't do anything about it
   b) sometimes cookies fall apart
   c) when bad things happen, you should be very upset

8) A few months after Peter fired Bob, his furniture store **went out of business**.
   a) started doing better
   b) moved to a different location
   c) closed

ANSWERS TO LESSON 22, p. 166

LESSON 23

BOB HAS A SURPRISE VISITOR

Bob's former boss Peter, from the furniture store, comes to visit. He offers Bob his old job back, but Bob's not interested.

Peter: Hi Bob. I was just in the neighborhood so I thought I'd **stop by**.

Bob: **Come on in**. Take a cookie.

Peter: Thanks. I'm glad to see you're not **holding a grudge against** me for firing you.

Bob: Not at all. **At first**, it **burned me up**. But I feel better now.

Peter: Good. I'm glad you have **no hard feelings**. How would you like your old job back?

Bob: What happened to your wonderful new manager?

Peter: She drank at work. By five o'clock, she'd be lying under a dining room table, **three sheets to the wind**. Yesterday, I finally **got rid of** her.

Bob: Let me **get this straight**. You replaced me with some crazy woman who **got plastered** every day **on the job**?

Peter: Yeah, I **lost my head**.

Bob: I don't think you lost your head. I just think you've got rocks in your head!

Peter: Bob, I'm trying to **level with you**. I never should've **let you go**.

Bob: **No use crying over spilt milk**.

Peter: So you'll come back and work for me?

Bob: **Not on your life!** Susan and I are very **well off** now. We just sold our new company for a **small fortune**!

IDIOMS – LESSON 23

at first – *see Lesson 16*

(to) burn someone up – to make someone angry

EXAMPLE 1: Jenny didn't vote for Nicole. That really **burns Nicole up**.
EXAMPLE 2: I can't believe Kristen and Andrew didn't invite us to their wedding. That really **burns me up**!

come on in – enter

EXAMPLE 1: **Come on in**, the door's open!
EXAMPLE 2: If nobody answers the door when you ring tonight, just **come on in**.

NOTE: This is a more conversational way of saying "come in."

(to) get plastered [slang] – to get drunk

EXAMPLE 1: Harold **got plastered** at the wedding and fell into the wedding cake.
EXAMPLE 2: That's your fifth martini. What are you trying to do, **get plastered**?

SYNONYMS: to get loaded [slang]; to get sloshed [slang]

(to) get rid of – to free oneself of; to throw out

EXAMPLE 1: We finally **got rid of** our spider problem, but now we have ants.
EXAMPLE 2: I've got too many old magazines and newspapers in my office. I need to **get rid of** some of them.

(to) get (something) straight – to clarify; to understand

EXAMPLE 1: Are you sure you **got the directions straight**?
EXAMPLE 2: Let me **get this straight** — you're leaving your husband?

(to) hold a grudge against (someone) – to stay angry with someone about a past offense

EXAMPLE 1: Nicole **holds a grudge against Jenny** for voting for Andrea instead of her.
EXAMPLE 2: Julia **held a grudge against her boyfriend** for not bringing her flowers on Valentine's Day.

(to) let (someone) go – to fire; dismiss employees

EXAMPLE 1: The investment bank **let Chris go** after they discovering he was stealing erasers, paper clips, and other office supplies.
EXAMPLE 2: The Xerxes Corporation was doing so poorly, they had to **let many workers go** earlier this year.

(to) level with (someone) – to speak openly and honestly with someone

EXAMPLE 1: Let me **level with you**. I'm voting for Andrea instead of you.
EXAMPLE 2: I have a feeling you're not telling me the whole truth. Please just **level with me**.

(to) lose one's head - to lose control of one's behavior; to not know what one is doing

EXAMPLE 1: Nicole **lost her head** after losing the elections and started yelling at all her friends.
EXAMPLE 2: Remember to stay calm before the judge. Don't get nervous and **lose your head**!

no hard feelings – no anger; no bitterness

EXAMPLE 1: After the elections, Andrea said to Nicole, "I hope there are **no hard feelings**."
EXAMPLE 2: I know you were disappointed that I beat you in the golf tournament, but I hope there are **no hard feelings**.

no use crying over spilt milk – there's no point in regretting something that's too late to change

EXAMPLE 1: Nicole realized she'd made some mistakes with her campaign for president, but there was **no use crying over spilt milk**.
EXAMPLE 2: Your bike was ruined in an accident? There's **no use crying over spilt milk**. You'll just have to buy a new one.

Not on your life! – definitely not

EXAMPLE 1: You want me to sit in that sauna for an hour? **Not on your life!**
EXAMPLE 2: Thanks for offering me a job in Siberia. Am I going to take it? **Not on your life!**

on the job – at work

EXAMPLE 1: Jennifer has four men **on the job** painting her house.
EXAMPLE 2: Dan got fired for drinking **on the job**.

small fortune – a good amount of money

EXAMPLE 1: When her great aunt died, Anne inherited a **small fortune**.
EXAMPLE 2: You won $25,000 in the lottery? That's a **small fortune**!

(to) stop by – to pay a quick visit

EXAMPLE 1: I'm having some friends over for pizza tomorrow night. Why don't you **stop by**?
EXAMPLE 2: **Stop by** my office on your way home tonight.

three sheets to the wind – drunk

EXAMPLE 1: After drinking four beers, Bob was **three sheets to the wind**.
EXAMPLE 2: Somebody needs to make sure Greg gets home safely. He's **three sheets to the wind**.

SYNONYMS: wasted [slang]; liquored up [slang]; dead drunk

well off – wealthy; financially secure

EXAMPLE 1: Betsy's grandfather used to be very **well off**, but he lost most of his fortune when the U.S. stock market crashed in 1929.
EXAMPLE 2: Debbie is a doctor and her husband is a lawyer. They're quite **well off**.

✎ PRACTICE THE IDIOMS

Choose the best substitute for the phrase or sentence in bold:

1) Nicole was very angry that she lost the election. Her mother told her **there was no use crying over spilt milk**.
   a) there was no point in feeling bad about what can't be changed
   b) she should think about all the mistakes she made
   c) maybe she could still change the results

2) Many people have died while climbing Mount Everest. Would I like to try it? **Not on your life!**
   a) Not if it means you'll be risking your life!
   b) Yes, definitely
   c) No way!

3) When Carol told Bob she could no longer sell Susan's Scrumptious Cookies, it really **burned him up**.
   a) made him feel happy
   b) made him feel sick
   c) made him very angry

4) Sara, I'm going to have to **let you go**. You come to work late every day and spend all day chatting with your friends.
   a) fire you
   b) give you more vacation time
   c) yell at you

5) One day, Nicole woke up with big red spots on her face. She didn't know how to **get rid of** them.
   a) make more of
   b) remove
   c) encourage

6) Thanks for coming to my party. **Come on in!**
   a) See you later!
   b) Go away!
   c) Enter!

7) Susan was **three sheets to the wind**. Bob told her not to drink any more piña coladas.
   a) really drunk
   b) very thirsty
   c) feeling very tired

8) Now that Bob is **well off**, he definitely won't be taking a job at McDonald's.
   a) employed
   b) feeling well
   c) secure financially

ANSWERS TO LESSON 23, p. 166

AMBER WRITES A SONG

Ted always writes the songs for the rock band. But now Amber says she wants to start writing songs too. She sings him the first lines of her new song.

Amber: Ted, you know how **all along** you've been **in charge of** all the lyrics for our band?

Ted: That's right, Amber. Everybody loves my songs!

Amber: Well, I hope they'll love my songs too.

Ted: But you don't write songs.

Amber: I'm **sick and tired of** singing your songs all the time. I want to sing my own songs!

Ted: Okay, no need to **freak out! First things first**. Have you written a song yet?

Amber: Yes, **as a matter of fact**, I have.

Ted: Well, let's hear it then.

Amber: Okay, but it's still a work **in progress**.

Ted: Stop trying to **buy time**. Let's hear the song!

Amber: ♪ My boyfriend is crazy. **Crazy about** baking cookies. I know **for sure** that there is no cure… ♪

Ted: **Cut it out**! Stop teasing me. I *am* cured.

Amber: **All better**?

Ted: Yes. I'll never bake another cookie again. My parents **made a fortune**. Now we can all just **chill out**!

IDIOMS – LESSON 24
all along – throughout; from beginning to end EXAMPLE 1: Jenny told Nicole she would vote for her, but **all along** she was planning on voting for Andrea. EXAMPLE 2: I never believed Joel when he told us he was marrying a princess from Denmark. I knew **all along** that he was lying.
all better – completely cured EXAMPLE 1: "**All better**?" asked Maureen, after her son stopped crying. EXAMPLE 2: If you're not **all better**, you shouldn't go to work tomorrow.
as a matter of fact – *see Lesson 20*
(to) buy (some) time – to make more time available (in order to achieve a certain purpose) EXAMPLE 1: We're not sure yet whether or not we want to buy the house. We'd better **buy some time** so we can think about it over the weekend. EXAMPLE 2: I'm not sure whether or not I want to take the job offer. I'd better **buy some time** to think about it.
(to) chill out [slang] – to relax EXAMPLE 1: **Chill out**! If we miss this train, we'll just take the next one. EXAMPLE 2: Your dog ate your homework? **Chill out**, I'm sure your teacher will understand!
(to be) crazy about – *see Lesson 5*

(to) cut it out – stop it; stop the annoying behavior

EXAMPLE 1: Tracy was chewing gum loudly during the movie. Her boyfriend finally told her to **cut it out**.
EXAMPLE 2: **Cut it out**! Stop trying to pull my shoes off!

first things first – let's focus on the most important thing or task first

EXAMPLE 1: You want to work here at Lulu's Dance Club? **First things first**, have you ever worked as a dancer before?
EXAMPLE 2: You want to ask your teacher if you can hand in your paper two weeks late? **First things first**, you'd better think of an excuse.

for sure – *see Lesson 19*

(to) freak out [slang] – to respond to something irrationally or crazily; to overreact

EXAMPLE 1: Ashley's parents **freaked out** when she told them she was dropping out of college to become an actress.
EXAMPLE 2: Don't **freak out** when I tell you this, but I lost the laptop you lent me last week.

(to be) in charge of – having responsibility for

EXAMPLE 1: John is **in charge of** all international sales for his company.
EXAMPLE 2: Who's **in charge of** making sure we don't run out of toilet paper in the bathroom?

in progress – happening; under way; going on now

EXAMPLE 1: The play is already **in progress**, so you'll have to wait until intermission to sit down.
EXAMPLE 2: Once the test is **in progress**, you will not be allowed to leave the room.

(to) make a fortune – to make a lot of money

EXAMPLE 1: Adam **made a fortune** when he sold his company to Microsoft.
EXAMPLE 2: Emma **made a fortune** selling candy to her classmates after lunch every day.

SYNONYMS: to make a bundle; to make a killing

(to be) sick and tired of – completely bored with; sick of

EXAMPLE 1: Ted is **sick and tired of** hearing about what an excellent student Nicole is.
EXAMPLE 2: I'm **sick and tired of** this nasty weather we've been having!

Fill in the blanks using these idioms:

buy time	**cut it out**
chill out	**in charge of**
freaked out	**sick and tired of**
all along	**first things first**

1) Nicole really _____ when she heard she lost the presidential election. She threw her books across the room!

2) Ted, why do you always leave your dirty clothes on the floor? Your mother is _____ cleaning up after you.

3) Donna, from the National Cookie Company, wanted Susan to sign a contract right away. Susan told her _____. She wanted to speak to a lawyer before signing any papers.

4) As president of the Spanish Club, Nicole will be _____ _____ organizing a trip to Spain in the spring.

5) When Nicole saw a group of her brother's friends laughing at her, she told them to _____.

6) After losing the election, Nicole was very upset. She needed to take it easy and _____.

7) Bob and Susan weren't sure yet how much they wanted to sell their cookie company for. They needed to _____ _____ so they could get some advice.

8) Nicole had assumed _____ that she was going to win the election. She was really surprised when she lost.

✪ Bonus Practice

Fill in the blank with the missing word:

1) Billy fell down the stairs and started crying. When he finally stopped, his mother asked, "All ____?"

   a) good   b) better   c) okay

2) Amber was happy when Ted said they didn't have to bake any more cookies. She was sick and tired ____ baking cookies.

   a) of   b) with   c) at

3) Ethan hasn't yet made up his mind whether or not to accept the job offer. He needs to ____ some time.

   a) buy   b) purchase   c) get

4) The man behind me on the train was whistling loudly. It was giving me a headache. Finally, I told him to ____ it out.

   a) stop   b) cut   c) sever

5) Chill ____! We're only going to be a few minutes late.

   a) it   b) in   c) out

6) Adam ____ a fortune working in computers in the late 90's. He was able to retire at age 39.

   a) had   b) made   c) found

7) The students were told that while the test was ____ progress, they wouldn't be allowed to leave the classroom.

   a) with   b) in   c) at

8) Victoria has a big job. She's in charge ____ the marketing department at her company.

   a) at   b) with   c) of

ANSWERS TO LESSON 24, p. 167

TED BRINGS HOME MORE GOOD NEWS

Ted tells his family that a talent agent wants to meet with him. The agent will fly Ted and Amber to New York. Nicole announces that she's been named president of the Spanish Club.

Ted: Amber and I are going to **break into** the music business. Last night after our concert, a talent agent asked us to meet with him in New York.

Susan: Congratulations! We'll give you some **spending money** for your trip.

Ted: No need. The agent is **footing the bill** for everything. And when we get there, he's going to **wine and dine** us.

Susan: He must think you're the **cream of the crop**.

Ted: He thinks we sound like the Goo Goo Dolls.

Nicole: Who are they?

Ted: You're really **out of it**. They're a popular rock band.

Nicole: Our family is certainly on a **winning streak**. I was elected president of the Spanish Club today.

Ted: The Spanish Club? **Big deal!**

Nicole: You don't **get it**, Ted. This is only the beginning. Today, president of the Spanish Club. Tomorrow, ambassador to Spain!

Ted: Well, Ambassador, you'll need to **wrap up** my chemistry homework before you leave for the Spanish Embassy.

Susan: A rock star and a diplomat — I'm so proud of both of you!

IDIOMS – LESSON 25

Big deal! – So what? That doesn't really matter.

EXAMPLE 1: You won five dollars in the lottery? **Big deal!**
EXAMPLE 2: Your father has a job with a big company in New York City? **Big deal!**

(to) break into – to enter or be let into a profession

EXAMPLE 1: If you want to **break into** journalism, it's a good idea to work on a college newspaper.
EXAMPLE 2: These days it's difficult to **break into** investment banking.

NOTE: "Break into" has several other meanings:
1. Interrupt. Boris and I were talking. Please don't try to **break into** our conversation.
2. Enter illegally or by force. Somebody **broke into** Peter's house and stole his DVD player.
3. To suddenly begin an activity, such as singing. After receiving the check from the National Cookie Company, Susan **broke into** song.

cream of the crop – the best of a group

EXAMPLE 1: In the world of women's tennis, the Williams sisters are the **cream of the crop**.
EXAMPLE 2: Of course you'll get accepted to Harvard. Don't forget, you're the **cream of the crop**!
SYNONYM: crème de la crème

(to) foot the bill – to pay

EXAMPLE 1: You paid last time we went to the movies. Let me **foot the bill** this time.
EXAMPLE 2: Fortunately, whenever we go out to dinner with the boss, she **foots the bill**.

SYNONYM: to pick up the tab

(to) get it – *see Lesson 21*

(to be) out of it – not aware or knowledgeable about trends or modern habits

EXAMPLE 1: Don't ask for Susan's advice on fashion. She's really **out of it**. She wears sneakers with everything.
EXAMPLE 2: Betsy has never even heard of Harry Potter. She's really **out of it**!

NOTE: "Out of it" also means "confused" or "disoriented." Example: After staying up all night studying, Ted felt **out of it** the next day.

spending money – money for minor expenses

EXAMPLE 1: Before Tim left for Europe, his parents gave him $400 in **spending money**.
EXAMPLE 2: Martin's parents are paying his college tuition, but he has to earn his own **spending money**.

SYNONYM: pocket money

(to) wine and dine – to take someone out for an evening or an expensive meal

EXAMPLE 1: Donna **wined and dined** Bob and Susan and then presented them with a contract for the sale of Susan's Scrumptious Cookies.
EXAMPLE 2: Kate was **wined and dined** during her trip to Santiago.

(to be on a) winning streak – a series of wins

EXAMPLE 1: The basketball team hasn't lost a game all season. They're on a **winning streak**!
EXAMPLE 2: You won 10 games in a row? You're on a **winning streak**!

(to) wrap up – to finish

EXAMPLE 1: If you **wrap up** your homework by eight o'clock, we'll have time to catch a movie tonight.
EXAMPLE 2: Okay folks, let's **wrap up** these exercises so we can go home early tonight.

✍ Practice the Idioms

Fill in the blank with the missing word:

1) I invited you to dinner, so let me ____ bill.

    a) hand off   b) arm   c) foot

2) My friend Kate is really ____ it. She doesn't even know who Oprah Winfrey is.

    a) out of   b) into   c) unaware of

3) Ted told Amber he'd need to call her back later in the evening since he was just ____ to have dinner.

    a) up   b) around   c) about

4) After Bob and Susan wrap ____ the sale of their business, they can relax for a while.

    a) through   b) around   c) up

5) Sally got a job with a law firm in Manhattan? ____ deal!

    a) Small   b) Big   c) Huge

6) We love to visit our friends in Florence, Italy. They always ____ and dine us.

    a) liquor   b) wine   c) beer

7) Bob and Susan plan to give Nicole $1,000 per year of spending ____ when she's in college.

    a) cash   b) dough   c) money

8) I recommend that you go to a concert at Carnegie Hall. The musicians who play there are always the cream of the ____.

    a) crop   b) lawn   c) lot

ANSWERS TO LESSON 25, p. 167

Review for Lessons 21-25

Fill in the blank with the missing word:

1) Next year, Ted will be traveling all ____ the world with his band.

    a) about   b) inside   c) over

2) After his fifth vodka, Steve was ____ sheets to the wind.

    a) five   b) three   c) two

3) For a while, the Johnsons were living ____ a shoestring. They couldn't afford to eat out at restaurants.

    a) with   b) on   c) by

4) When my friend lost her favorite necklace, I told her it was no use crying over spilt ____.

    a) milk   b) juice   c) beer

5) Joel has a fun job. He's ____ charge of advertising sales for *Mad,* the best humor magazine in America.

    a) at   b) on   c) in

6) Please put away your wallet! Let me ____ the bill.

    a) arm   b) foot   c) hand

7) My friend was running around like a chicken with its head cut off. I told her to chill ____.

    a) out   b) in   c) down

8) Bob worked out the nuts and _____ of the agreement with the National Cookie Company.

    a) details   b) bolts   c) tacks

9) After Martha's neighbor chopped down her apple tree, she held a grudge _____ him for years.

    a) from   b) against   c) for

10) I arrived late to the stadium. The baseball game was already _____ progress.

    a) through   b) in   c) at

11) My friend invited me out for a drink, but I told her I'd first need to wrap _____ some things at the office.

    a) through   b) along   c) up

12) I'm _____ and tired of telemarketers calling me in the evening trying to sell me stuff I don't want.

    a) sick   b) ill   c) angry

13) Kristen's boss paid her a compliment. He said she was the best salesperson in the company. That really _____ her day.

    a) made   b) created   c) ruined

14) The person seated behind me on the airplane kept on kicking my seat. Finally, I told him to _____ it out.

    a) stop   b) cut   c) fly

15) Amber hopes to break _____ the modeling business after she graduates from high school. She can definitely model nose rings and tattoos!

    a) into   b) in   c) around

CROSSWORD PUZZLE

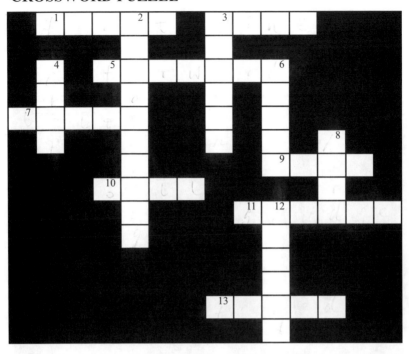

Across

1. First things ____. Before we start wandering around the streets of Paris, let's look at a map and plan our route.
3. The company will wine and ____ their top candidates for this position.
5. Nicole was really looking ____ to her school trip to Spain.
7. Ken is an engineer. He tries to understand the nuts and ____ of how things work.
9. When the stock market collapsed, Bob lost his ____ and sold everything.
10. Nicole's boyfriend forgot his wallet, so she had to foot the ____.
11. Bob no longer shops at the Village Market. He holds a ____ against them.
13. I was sick and ____ of watching my co-worker flirt with our boss.

Down

2. We can't afford a new computer for the office. We're running on a ____.
3. Bette Davis may have been a great actress, but she was a ____ lady in real life.
4. Musicians from the Juilliard School of Music are the cream of the ____.
6. Diane and Mike just bought a mansion. They're rolling in ____.
8. Mary left her husband George for a younger man. She told George, "I hope there are no ____ feelings about this."
12. Stephen King has a long track ____ of writing bestsellers.

ANSWERS TO REVIEW, p. 167

CHALLENGE CROSSWORD PUZZLE

How well have you learned the idioms in this book? This crossword puzzle will test you. Idioms are taken from throughout the entire book. If you can solve the whole puzzle, *good for you!*

Across

2. The US team did not win the World Cup, but they gave it their best _____.
3. You think Al should tell his boss that she's wrong? Easier said than _____!
4. The English teacher gave her students a useful _____ of thumb. She told them not to repeat the same adjectives too many times in one essay.
6. You have an exam tomorrow morning? You'd better start hitting the _____!
7. Todd doesn't like reading. It's like _____ teeth to get him to read anything.
11. Julie was very upset when her landlord increased her rent by 25 percent. Now she doesn't know how she'll make ends _____.
14. Eva loves to travel. She's traveled all _____ the world.
15. Stop jumping up and down on the bed! If it breaks, it'll be no laughing _____.
16. I wanted to buy *The New York Times* this morning, but by the time I got to the store, they had already _____ out.
18. Good luck at the casino. Hopefully you'll strike it _____!
23. Jay didn't cheat during the Scrabble game. He won _____ and square.
24. You look very tired. We'd better call it a _____ and go home.
25. You paid $900 for that cappuccino maker? That's really _____ dollar!
28. You're going on vacation to Aruba? I'm _____ with envy.

Down

1. On a hot day like today, an ice cream stick is just what the _____ ordered!
2. We've only got two hours to finish this project. Let's roll up our _____ and start working.
3. Pfizer really wanted to Tanya to accept their job offer, so they agreed to sweeten the _____ .
5. If you studied your idioms, this crossword puzzle should be a _____ of cake.
8. Ted_____ around the bush before telling his parents that he failed his test.
9. Mmmm, this chocolate cake is out of this _____!
10. Joe wants to join the army, but he hasn't yet broken the _____ to his mom.
11. Oh, you're finally home. That's a load off my _____!
12. Frank, our best salesman, hasn't made a sale all week. I'm afraid he's lost his _____!
13. Mark drove a hard _____ and got two T-shirts for the price of one.
17. Vivian is a night _____. She never goes to sleep before midnight.
19. I know you had your _____ set on going skiing this weekend, but I'm afraid there won't be enough snow.
20. You'd better get up _____ and early to finish your homework.
21. Your team won four soccer games in a row? You're on a _____ streak.
22. All of Brianna's after-school activities cost money. Her parents are tired of shelling _____ so much money.
23. Judy made a list of books for the book club to read, but she told members to feel _____ to make other suggestions.
26. Will Democrats and Republicans every stop fighting? When _____ fly!
27. Tom doesn't want to go to the rock concert. Jazz is more his cup of _____.

ANSWERS TO PUZZLE, p. 168

159

hit the nail on the head gung ho come to an agreement in that case stand a cha~~nce~~ ~~fl~~y hang around cup of tea make ~~the goods get~~ the ball rolling ~~onal wisdom take~~ something by storm burn the midnight oil no laughing matter

ANSWER KEY

LESSON 1: BOB'S DAY AT WORK

1. b	5. b
2. a	6. a
3. c	7. c
4. a	8. c

LESSON 2: BOB RETURNS HOME WITH BAD NEWS

1. c	5. a
2. b	6. c
3. c	7. a
4. c	8. b

LESSON 3: TED'S DAY AT SCHOOL

1. c	5. c
2. a	6. a
3. a	7. b
4. b	8. a

LESSON 4: NICOLE'S DAY AT SCHOOL

1. b	5. c
2. c	6. a
3. b	7. c
4. b	8. a

BONUS PRACTICE

1. c	4. b
2. a	5. c
3. b	6. b

LESSON 5: TED GOES OUT FOR THE EVENING

1. b	5. a
2. a	6. b
3. c	7. b
4. b	8. c

REVIEW: LESSONS 1-5

1. b	5. b	9. c	13. c
2. b	6. a	10. a	14. b
3. c	7. b	11. b	15. b
4. c	8. c	12. a	

```
            C
      M A T T E R
            N
  C H I N N
  O     E
  M I N D
  P             L
B L O W     C R E E P S
  I         U   G
  M         T
  E   B O O K S
  N   A
  T A C K
      K
```

LESSON 6: SUSAN STAYS HOME & BAKES COOKIES

1. a	5. b
2. b	6. b
3. c	7. a
4. c	8. a

LESSON 7: SUSAN HIRES BOB TO RUN HER BUSINESS

1. b	5. b
2. a	6. c
3. c	7. a
4. a	8. c

LESSON 8: TED FORMS A ROCK BAND

1. a	5. b
2. a	6. b
3. c	7. b
4. a	8. c

LESSON 9: NICOLE FOR PRESIDENT!

1. b   5. a
2. a   6. c
3. b   7. b
4. c   8. a

LESSON 10: BOB VISITS THE VILLAGE MARKET

1. c   5. a
2. b   6. a
3. a   7. c
4. b   8. a

REVIEW: LESSONS 6-10

1. c   5. b   9. b
2. a   6. a   10. b
3. c   7. c
4. b   8. a

LESSON 11: BOB DRIVES A HARD BARGAIN

Abe: Hi, Jeff. <u>How's it going</u>?

Jeff: Fine, thanks. I've only scheduled a half hour for this meeting, so we'd better <u>get the ball rolling</u>.

Abe: Jeff, I need you to come up with a new advertising campaign for my furniture shop.

Jeff: I've had a chance to <u>crunch some numbers,</u> and you'll need to pay me $30,000 to come up with some new ideas.

Abe: Thirty thousand dollars? That's really <u>out of the question</u>!

Jeff: Listen, Abe, I need to <u>make a living</u> too. I've got a wife and seven children at home.

Abe: I'll pay you $20,000.

Jeff: If you want quality work, you have to pay for it. Let's say $25,000?

Abe: Okay, okay. You've <u>twisted my arm</u>. I'll pay you $23,000.

Jeff: <u>Now you're talking</u>. That's a fair price.

Abe: You certainly <u>drive a hard bargain</u>.

Jeff: I know, but you'll be happy with my work.

LESSON 12: BOB'S BIG COOKIE ORDER

1. a	5. b
2. b	6. c
3. a	7. a
4. b	8. c

BONUS PRACTICE

1. c	4. a
2. a	5. b
3. c	6. b

LESSON 13: AMBER COMES OVER TO BAKE COOKIES

1. c	5. b
2. c	6. a
3. a	7. a
4. b	8. b

LESSON 14: AMBER AND TED HEAT UP THE KITCHEN

I met Bob in college. He was in my English Literature class. I liked him right away. For me, it was <u>love at first sight</u>. I wrote him several love poems, though I never gave them to him. Then I found out he had a girlfriend. I saw him <u>making out</u> with a girl named Joyce. It looked like she was <u>crazy about</u> Bob too. But later that week, I heard that she was a nasty person and that she <u>treated him like dirt</u>. So I decided to <u>go ahead</u> and ask him to the movies. He said he was too busy. It was <u>crunch time</u>, and he had to <u>crank out</u> a paper for literature class and study for several exams. But I didn't give up. I kept <u>plugging away</u>. Then one day he <u>broke up with</u> Joyce and asked me out to dinner. That was 25 years ago, and we're still together. Fortunately, we're still <u>head over heels in love</u> with each other!

LESSON 15: NICOLE PRACTICES HER ELECTION SPEECH

1. b	4. a	7. c
2. a	5. b	8. a
3. c	6. b	

REVIEW: LESSONS 11-15

1. a	5. a	9. b
2. c	6. a	10. b
3. b	7. b	11. b
4. c	8. c	12. a

LESSON 16: BOB BRINGS THE COOKIES TO THE VILLAGE MARKET

1. b
2. b
3. c
4. c
5. b
6. a
7. b
8. c

LESSON 17: CAROL TELLS BOB THE GOOD NEWS

1. a
2. b
3. a
4. b
5. b
6. c
7. a
8. c

LESSON 18: EVERYONE BAKES COOKIES

1. c
2. b
3. c
4. a
5. b
6. c
7. a
8. b

BONUS PRACTICE

1. c
2. a
3. c
4. b
5. b
6. a
7. c
8. b

LESSON 19: NICOLE'S CLOSE ELECTION

Ted: Nicole, my teacher gave me back my chemistry homework. I got a terrible grade! I thought <u>for sure</u> you'd help me get an "A+."

Nicole: I'm sorry. I really did <u>give it my best shot</u>, but I guess it wasn't good enough.

Ted: Not good enough? That's right. You really <u>messed up</u>!

Nicole: You never should've asked me to do your homework. Don't try to <u>put the blame on me</u> for your bad grades.

Ted: Yes, my mistake. I thought you were a <u>sure thing</u>!

Nicole: So you'll get a bad grade in chemistry. Just learn to <u>live with it</u>. Here, take one of Mom's cookies. It'll help <u>cheer you up</u>.

Ted: You think a stupid cookie will cheer me up? <u>Give me a break</u>!

LESSON 20: BOB GETS AN ANGRY CALL FROM CAROL

1. a
2. b
3. a
4. c
5. b
6. c
7. b
8. b

REVIEW: LESSONS 16-20

1. c	5. b	9. a
2. b	6. a	10. a
3. c	7. c	
4. a	8. b	

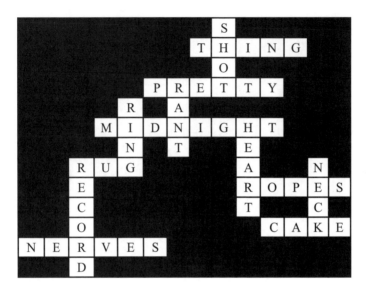

LESSON 21: SUSAN GETS A SURPRISE CALL

1. c	5. b
2. c	6. a
3. a	7. b
4. c	8. a

LESSON 22: SUSAN SHARES THE GOOD NEWS

1. c	5. a
2. b	6. b
3. a	7. a
4. b	8. c

LESSON 23: BOB HAS A SURPRISE VISITOR

1. a	5. b
2. c	6. c
3. c	7. a
4. a	8. c

LESSON 24: AMBER WRITES A SONG

1. freaked out
2. sick and tired of
3. first things first
4. in charge of
5. cut it out
6. chill out
7. buy time
8. all along

BONUS PRACTICE

1. b
2. a
3. a
4. b
5. c
6. b
7. b
8. c

LESSON 25: TED BRINGS HOME MORE GOOD NEWS

1. c
2. a
3. c
4. c
5. b
6. b
7. c
8. a

REVIEW: LESSONS 21-25

1. c
2. b
3. b
4. a
5. c
6. b
7. a
8. b
9. b
10. b
11. c
12. a
13. a
14. b
15. a

CHALLENGE CROSSWORD PUZZLE

A

about to, 12
after all, 12
all along, 146
all better (to be), 146
all over, 130

all the rage, 82
as a matter of fact, 122
at first, 102
at least, 12

B

ballpark figure, 64
basket case, 94
beat around the bush, 52
beside the point, 24
better off, 134
big deal!, 152
big head, 94
big shot, 112
bite off more than one can chew, 76
blow it, 106
blow something, 24
blow things out of proportion, 122
break into, 152

break the news, 13
break up with someone, 88
brown-noser, 58
bright and early, 48
buckle down, 24
burn someone up, 140
burn the midnight oil, 106
butt in, 28
buy out, 134
buy time, 146
by a hair, 118
by far, 58

C

call it a night, 82
can't complain, 72
can't stand, 24
change one's mind, 18
cheer someone up, 42
chill out, 146
chitchat, 106
cold shoulder (to give someone the), 59
come on in, 140
come to an agreement, 130
conventional wisdom, 94

cost an arm and a leg, 13
count on someone, 59
crank out, 88
crash course, 48
crazy about, 34
cream of the crop, 152
crunch numbers, 72
crunch time, 88
cup of tea, 34
cut class, 24
cut it out, 147

D

dead end job, 13
deliver the goods, 106
dime a dozen, 52
do one's best, 106
do the trick, 95
don't mention it, 64

down in the dumps, 34
dragon lady, 134
drive a hard bargain, 72
drive one crazy, 28
drop by, 34

E

easier said than done, 18

F

face it, 13
fair and square, 118
fat chance, 48
feel free, 83
figure out, 64
find out, 122
first things first, 147

fool around, 112
foot the bill, 153
for heaven's sake, 76
for sure, 118
freak out, 147
from scratch, 64
full of oneself, 59

G

get a handle on, 123
get canned, 18
get down to business, 59
get going, 76
get it, 134
get on one's nerves, 112
get one's act together, 123
get out of the way, 83
get plastered, 140
get real, 24
get rid of, 140
get something straight, 141
get the ball rolling, 72
get the hang of something, 102
get the show on the road, 112
get under one's belt, 59
give someone credit, 42
give credit where credit is due, 42
give it a shot, 48
give it one's best shot, 118

give me a break, 88
give one the creeps, 13
give someone a ring, 102
give someone a run for his money, 59
give someone the ax, 13
give someone the cold shoulder, 59
give someone the time of day, 60
give up, 118
go ahead, 89
go back to the drawing board, 13
go belly up, 13
go into, 28
go into business, 42
go nuts, 64
go wrong, 119
good for you, 53
good thinking, 42
goody-goody, 60
green with envy, 28
gung ho, 28

H

hang around, 34
hang in there, 18
hang out, 34
happy camper, 49
hard times, 53
have a blast, 35
have a good time, 35
have one's heart set on, 24
have under one's belt, 59

head and shoulders above, 28
head over heels in love, 89
heart of gold (to have a), 42
help out, 76
help yourself, 43
hit the books, 24
hit the nail on the head, 29
hold a grudge against someone, 141
how's it going?, 72

I

if worst comes to worst, 18
I'll say, 95
in a bad mood, 43
in any case, 102
in charge of, 147
in good hands, 83
in good spirits, 53

in person, 102
in progress, 147
in reality, 95
in that case, 130
in touch with, 130
it looks like, 135
it's a deal, 60

J

jump the gun, 65
just kidding, 65
just what the doctor ordered, 43

K

keep one's chin up, 19
keep posted, 102
kid around, 60

knock oneself out, 123
know one's stuff, 83

L

last resort, 19
learn the ropes, 103
lend a hand, 83
let someone go, 141
level with someone, 141
lighten up, 112
like a chicken with its head cut off, 77
like crazy, 77
like pulling teeth, 77
live from hand to mouth, 19

live with it, 119
load off one's mind, 95
look forward to, 131
look like, 95
look on the bright side, 19
lose one's head, 141
lose one's temper, 14
lose one's touch, 83
lost cause, 25
love at first sight, 89

M

made of money, 53
make a bundle, 43
make a fool of oneself, 119
make a fortune, 147
make a living, 73
make a pig of oneself, 65
make a splash, 53

make ends meet, 19
make one's day, 131
make out, 89
make time for, 65
make up one's mind, 14
mess up, 119
mixed feelings, 49

N

needless to say, 49
nervous wreck, 95
never mind, 77
night owl, 113
no hard feelings, 141
no laughing matter, 135
no point in, 14
not give a hoot, 25
not give someone the time of day, 60
not have a clue, 49

not sleep a wink, 49
no wonder, 95
no use crying over spilt milk, 141
not on your life!, 142
nothing doing!, 113
nothing to do with, 135
now you're talking, 73
nuts about, 89
nuts and bolts, 131

O

on a shoestring, 131
on edge, 43
on the job, 142
on thin ice with someone, 29
one's heart goes out to someone, 123
one-track mind, 89

out of it, 153
out of practice, 83
out of the question, 73
out of this world, 43
out of work, 19
over one's head, 25

P

pain in the neck, 103
pay someone back, 53
pay someone a compliment, 29
pick up, 84
piece of cake, 103
pig out, 43

pipe dream, 53
pitch in, 77
plug away (at something), 90
pull an all-nighter, 96
put the blame on someone, 119
put up with, 14

R

rant and rave, 123
real flop, 14
rest assured, 107
right away, 107
right-hand man, 19

roll up one's sleeves, 65
rolling in dough, 135
round up, 103
rule of thumb, 96
run around, 77

S

save the day, 14
second nature, 103
sell like hotcakes, 107
set eyes on, 20
set the record straight, 119
shake in one's shoes, 29
sharp as a tack, 14
shell out, 54
shut up, 29
sick and tired of, 147
sit tight, 65
sitting pretty, 107
slack off, 25

small fortune, 142
sold out, 107
spending money, 153
stab someone in the back, 20
stand a chance, 25
stay up, 113
stop by, 142
stressed out, 20
strike it rich, 135
sure thing, 119
sweep something under the rug, 123
sweet tooth, 84
sweeten the deal, 73

T

take a break, 84
take it easy, 35
take it or leave it, 73
take off, 107
take over, 84
take something by storm, 54
take something the wrong way, 35
taken aback, 124
talk into, 60
talk over, 14
tall order, 107
tell off, 20
thank goodness, 20
that's the way the cookie crumbles, 135

the breaks (those are *or* that's), 54
there's no accounting for taste, 35
things are looking up, 77
think big, 20
three sheets to the wind, 142
throw the book at someone, 124
to tell you the truth, 103
too many cooks spoil the broth, 84
top dollar, 14
track record, 131
treat someone like dirt, 90
tricks of the trade, 84
turn off, 96
twist someone's arm, 73

U

under one's breath, 35
up in the air, 35

W

way to go!, 29
well off, 142
what's the matter?, 20
what's up?, 65
when pigs fly, 20
wine and dine, 153
winning streak, 153

wise guy, 54
work like a dog, 49
work one's tail off, 84
work out, 131
worth one's while, 73
wrap up, 153

Y

you can say that again, 65
you scratch my back and I'll scratch yours, 60
your guess is as good as mine, 103

LANGUAGE SUCCESS PRESS INTRODUCES...

LOSE YOUR ACCENT IN 28 DAYS

Book + CD-ROM + Audio CD = A Complete System!

Lose Your Accent in 28 Days is a new system that will help you get rid of your foreign accent forever. Practice just 30 minutes a day for one month, and you'll change the way you speak English. No more being asked to repeat yourself. No more feeling embarrassed by your accent. Imagine how much more confident you'll feel!

 Accent Reduction Specialist Judy Ravin has spent the last 10 years helping foreign nationals lose their foreign accents. Her clients have included thousands of business executives, including many from Fortune 500 companies. Judy and her accent reduction system have been featured on *National Public Radio*. Now you too can benefit from her innovative system of accent reduction. This three-in-one system brings Judy right to you.

- ☑ On the **CD-ROM**, Judy will show you on video exactly how to form your mouth to make difficult vowel and consonant sounds. If you're currently using a system without this important video component, you're missing the picture!
- ☑ On the **audio CD**, you'll join Judy and her training team in practicing the additional aspects of perfect pronunciation: rhythm, stress, and intonation. Listen, repeat, and master.
- ☑ In the **workbook**, you'll follow along with the CD-ROM and audio CD and learn additional techniques for making sounds correctly and getting rid of your accent.

ORDER ONLINE:
www.languagesuccesspress.com

LANGUAGE SUCCESS PRESS

ABOUT LANGUAGE SUCCESS PRESS

Language Success Press is a publishing house based in Ann Arbor, Michigan, USA. We were founded in 2002. Our mission is to help people all over the world improve their conversational English skills. Our focus is on *American* English. We want our readers to enjoy the learning process – that's why we always use interesting stories and examples. All of our authors have experience teaching English as a Second Language (ESL) so they understand the challenges of mastering conversational English!

Our products include:

- **Speak English Like an American**: versions for native Spanish speakers, native Japanese speakers, native Russian speakers and this all-English version.

- **Lose Your Accent in 28 Days**: a new multimedia learning system designed to help people lose their foreign accents forever. This set consists of a workbook, a CD-ROM, and an audio CD.

- **Language Wheels**: spinning these wheels provides a fun and effective way to practice grammar and build vocabulary. Four types of wheels are available: Adjectives, Adverbs and Nouns; Irregular Verbs; Phrasal Verbs; and Business Phrasal Verbs.

Visit our website to find out about new
releases & to order our products.
We offer special discounts online!
www.languagesuccesspress.com

NOTES